THE PRIVATE EYE ANNUAL 2002

EDITED BY IAN HISLOP

Published in Great Britain by
Private Eye Productions Ltd
6 Carlisle Street, London W1D 5BN

© 2002 Pressdram Ltd
ISBN 1 901784 282
Designed by Bridget Tisdall
Printed in England by
Ebenezer Baylis & Son Ltd, Worcester

2 4 6 8 10 9 7 5 3 1

THE PRIVATE EYE ANNUAL 2002

EDITED BY IAN HISLOP

THE WAR ON TERRORISM
THE STORY IN PICTURES

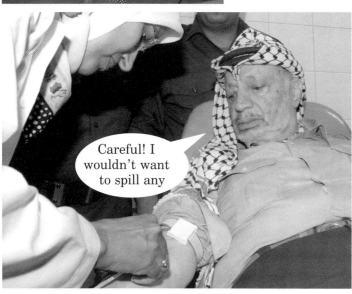

"To whom it may concern..."

DECLARATION OF WAR

Austin

WORLD WAR THREE

GOOD WILL TRIUMPH OVER EVIL

It's Official!

By Our Entire Staff B.L. ZEBUB

THE whole world was immensely reassured today when President George W. Bush announced that good will triumph over evil.

For centuries, philosophers and theologians have been engaged in anguished debate on this issue, and there has been considerable doubt, as the philosopher Spinoza put it, "which way the cookie is going to crumble".

Universal Relief

Following President Bush's categorical statements, stock markets recovered, old age pensioners danced in the streets and millions of terrorists rushed to hand in their weapons in the knowledge that, metaphysically speaking, as the great philosopher Kant once put it they were in a "no-win situation".

NO WORDS CAN DESCRIBE THIS OUTRAGE

Pages 1, 2, 3, 4, 5, 6, 7, 8, 9, 10, 11, 12, 15, 16, 17, 20, 21, 32, 33, 36, 21, 26, 27, 28, 31, 46, 60, 51, 58, 40, 41, 44, 45, 46, 65, 68, 69, 59, 63, 64, 65...

Ken Pyne

New York attack was foreseen by Nostradamus

by Mirror Staff **Phillipa Page**

THE ATTACK on the twin towers of the World Trade Center was precisely predicted in every detail more than 400 years ago by the French seer Nostradamus.

In 1559 he wrote:

Where two rivers meet, in the land of the giant mouse,
There shall be fire in the sky,
and a bush will be seen underground.

Says mediaeval scholar **Professor Fantoni** of the Department of Horoscopology at the University of Legova, Italy:

"Nostradamus's astonishingly prescient couplet begins with a clear reference to the meeting of New York's two rivers, which is exactly where the World Trade Center used to stand. He then continues, lest there be any doubt as to which country is being referred to, with an unmistakable allusion to Disneyworld in Florida, with its more-than-life-size emblem of Mickey, the 'giant mouse' cited by Nostradamus. Most astonishing of all is Nostradamus's vision of President Bush retiring to his underground command bunker in Nebraska."

NEXT WEEK: How Nostradamus foresaw Iain Duncan Smith becoming elected as leader of the Tory Party.

GEORGE WW3 BUSH

nem.

WORLD WAR THREE

What You Didn't Miss

Day One (on all channels)

Presenter *(putting on serious face)*: It's obviously much too early to speculate, but we have in the studio several experts who are going to try to help us to get some idea of this almost unimaginable tragedy, which is already being described as the worst thing that has happened in the world since the death of Princess Diana.

Professor Ivan Beard, you run the Terrorist Studies Department at the University of Inverneasden. Who do you think is responsible for this appalling tragedy that is already being spoken of as the worst thing that has happened to the world since Hiroshima?

Beard: Well, it's obviously too early to speculate. But I think we have to look at all the various groups who might be capable of doing something like this. And I'm sure that's what the various intelligence agencies will be doing over the next few days and weeks, as they attempt to piece together the various pieces of this incredibly complex jigsaw.

Presenter: Can we just see the footage again of the plane going into that tower?

(Film runs in slow motion for 42nd time in previous hour)

Presenter: And obviously as we are watching that our thoughts go to all the families and loved ones of the victims, and we shall be interviewing some of them later as they try to come to terms with this almost unimaginable tragedy which is already being compared to... er... General Sir Michael Bore, could I bring you in here on the military aspects of this story. Obviously the United States will have to retaliate in some way. What form do you think that will take?

Bore: Well, it's obviously too early to speculate, but I think it's important, before launching any strike, to have some clear idea of just who you're going to attack. It's no good just firing off a load of cruise missiles unless you have some idea of the target. That's one thing we learned in Kosovo, and I'm sure my friend Colin Powell will be very well aware of that.

Presenter: Can we have the footage of that first tower collapsing again, please?

(Film runs in slow motion for 86th time in previous hour)

Presenter: Joe Talbott, you're the London bureau chief for Newstalk magazine. You know New York well. What do you think will be the feeling in New York as people come to terms with this horrifying tragedy?

Talbott: Well, it's still too early to speculate, but I would suggest that the predominant feelings of most ordinary New Yorkers as of this time would be a combination of shock, disbelief, and sheer disbelieving shock. This is a city, you have to remember, which did not go through the Blitz, like you people in London. I was talking just now to a friend in Manhattan, who told me that there is an uncanny feeling just now of shocked disbelief.

Presenter: Do we have any clear idea yet of the likely number of casualties?

Talbott: Well, the latest word from Mayor Giuliani is that it's too early speculate.

Presenter: Yes, of course, but all the evidence suggests that we're looking at hundreds of thousands. Who do you think we should blame for this? Is it Osram Bin Liner, the world's most evil man? Professor?

Beard: Well, Bin Liner must obviously be a prime suspect. But the question is, does he have the capability? In my own view, he does, but I would have to qualify that by saying that I really don't know. But one thing that I think we can say is certain is that it is something the intelligence agencies will be looking at very carefully indeed over the next hours and days, as they struggle to come to terms with what is being spoken of as the worst thing that has ever happened in the history of the world.

Presenter: Thank you, professor. And now, can we have some more footage of people jumping out of windows? *(cont. on all channels)*

Extremists Seen Dancing And Cheering In Guardian

by Our Media Staff **Roy Greenslime**

FANATICAL anti-American supporters of the sinister leader Al-Rubbisha were seen openly celebrating in the offices of the Guardian newspaper at the news that the World Trade Centre had been attacked.

Rubbisha was quick to deny the charge, saying "Only a small proportion of my columnists, ie 80%, were involved in the singing and dancing. The rest showed their respect by having a 3-minute sing-song of 'America The Bastards'."

"If only I could go to Paradise with you – but, alas, I'm needed here on Earth"

THAT HISTORIC BUSH SPEECH IN FULL

MAH fellow Americans. Words fail me at this terrible time. So let's have a moment of silence while I think of something to say.

(Man hands him piece of paper)

Mah fellow Americans. Look solemn and read this out slowly. Ours is a nation based on freedom and democracy. These folks who live on the hill... no, that's a song. But it's an American song, and it's one I'm proud to sing. These folks who flew these planes into our American buildings had better know that we're going to seek them out wherever they may be, and bring them to justice. And of course democracy and freedom. They are cowardly men, who run away at the first sign of danger. I'm sorry, I've got to go now to my security bunker in Nebraska. But if any of these folks turn up here, don't tell them where I've gone.

God bless Arabia.

© G. W. Bush 2001.

DAILY NEWSCARE

WE MUST NOT GIVE IN TO TERROR

BLAIR RECALLS PARLIAMENT

*I remember now...
...it's the place where I tell people what to do*

On Other Pages

Bin Laden has nuclear weapons . **2**

Nerve gas attack imminent **3**

Britain is terrorists' main target . **4**

Global recession now definite . . **5**

House prices will tumble **6**

We're all going to die **94**

Exclusive To All Newspapers

TRAPPED IN THE DARK AGES PREPARING FOR BATTLE

by Our Reporter Inside Afghanistan
WILL THISMAKEMEFAMOUS

AFTER three days' journeying, clad in traditional Arab garb so as to pass unnoticed through countless Taliban checkpoints, I reached the ancient village of Abdurazek, a town in a state of raw nervousness and mediaeval squalor.

I crossed a square of shops, where the only thing on sale seemed to be the fear that clung to every doorway. There I approached a young girl of no more than ten, her head shrouded in a veil, standing nervously by a well that had long since dried up under this repressive regime.

"Are you apprehensive about the American military strikes to come?" I asked.

In a trembling voice, whose courage will live with me forever, she replied, "No, I'm John Simpson in disguise. Go away, you twat."

Surely this message to the world from these simple, brave, people show a determination and spirit that cannot be... *(Cont. p. 94)*

Dave Spartby, Editor of the *New Spartsman* magazine, writes:

I SEE no reason to apologise for my totally reasonable editorial in which I said that the attack on the so-called World Trade Center was a perfectly reasonable response to the sickening terrorism of American capitalism and er that the bond dealers and yuppies who died totally deserved their fate due to their failure to vote for the non-Fascist non-Bush candidate in the so-called US elections and er... the unfortunate fact that the twin towers were actually full of low-paid immigrant insurance clerks in no way invalidates my central theory that er... anyway my views are totally consistent with the New Spartsman magazine which is a totally independent publication owned by the sickening capitalist Geoffrey Robinson and is therefore a legitimate target for a terrorist attack, er...

What He May Look Like Now

THE world's top intelligence experts believe that the world's most wanted terrorist Osama bin Liner will by now have had a complete make-over. He will almost certainly have shaved off his beard, put on a pair of heavy-framed glasses and adopted a bogus upper-English accent. The picture above shows a CIA computer-generated image of what Bin Liner now looks like.

HELLO!

NUMBER 1038 ● OCTOBER 5, 2001 ● £1.20

TOP WORLD TERRORIST OZZY BIN LADEN WELCOMES US INTO HIS CAVE

THE handsome bearded face creased into a smile. "I never thought you'd find me," joked the world's most famous terrorist, Osama "Ozzy" Bin Laden, as he proudly showed me round his new cave.

"I've only been here a couple of hours," he said, "but already it's home."

Osama is delightfully down-to-earth, despite his status as the world's No.1 celebrity mass-murderer.

His charming cave is tastefully decorated with Afghan wall-hangings and state-of-the-art ground-to-air missile systems.

Any reader of Hello! might envy Ozzy's simple lifestyle in his remote hideaway, with its breathtaking views of distant snow-capped mountains and smiling peasants being strung up from lamp-posts by the Taliban.

I asked him first whether he ever got lonely, in his dedicated mission to destroy the civilised world.

"Allah is good to me," he said, with a shy smile, referring to the world's most famous Islamic divinity, whom Bin Laden regards as a close friend.

"But don't you miss your 529 brothers and sisters?" I asked.

"We keep in touch via the newspapers," he explained, "where they can read about me every day."

"It must be very difficult for you, being so rich and famous," I suggested. "Doesn't the pressure ever get to you?"

"No," he smiled, "because I enjoy using my wealth and my fame to do bad in the world."

I thanked this shy star of the world stage for giving up the time to talk to us, and opening his heart to us in such a delightful fashion.

© HELLO! MAGAZINE

THAT HISTORIC BUSH SPEECH IN FULL

MAH fellow Americans... ask not what your country can do for you... I have a dream... we shall fight them on the television... we hold these truths to be self-evident... oh what a beautiful morning... an iron curtain has descended... veni vidi vici... they shall not grow old... zippideedooda... never in the field of human conflict was so much effort made by so many to find so few... ich bin ein Binliner... that's all folks...

(Standing ovation... senators weep... Bush hailed as greatest statesman since his dad.)

HOW TO TELL A TERRORIST FROM A MEMBER OF THE WORLDWIDE COALITION AGAINST TERRORISM

Genuine Terrorist

Genuine Friend of Democracy

GLENDA SLAGG

Fleet Street's Biological Weapon!

● HATS OFF to feisty Anne Robinson!?!!

She's opened her soul to the world and made us laugh and weep with her bittersweet memoirs of being a mum, a boozer and the world's biggest-ever TV star!?!

What a role-model for all the women of the world!?!

She's a red-head, red-hot, hard-drinkin', hard-lovin', hard-livin' Mama!?!

Question: Who is the strongest link? *Answer:* You are, Annie!! (Geddit?!!)

● OK, SO SHE drank eight bottles of vodka a day and woke up in some strange bloke's bed covered in vomit?!?! Who hasn't?!

We're not living in Afghanistan, Annie – that's life for all of us gals living in 2001!?!

Stop cashin' in on your drinking, your daughter, and your dreary husbands!?!

Here's a tip from Auntie Glenda (who's been there, done it and been sick on the t-shirt!?!) – Annie, Get Your Gun and shoot yourself!?!

Goodbye!!

● *HATS and everything else off to 93-year-old Joan Collins!?! Let's hear it for a gal who's not afraid to go a-dancin' and a-prancin' in her knickers when she should be in a geriatric ward!?!!*

But what a trouper!?!? They don't make stars like her any more!?!? If we want to win the war in Afghanistan, we should send out our Joanie in her suspenders!?!? And watch the Taliban run for cover!?!?

● TALKING of the Taliban, am I the only one who has got the hots for Osama bin Laden?!? *(No. This piece has been in every other paper. Ed.)*

With his dark brown eyes, silky beard and smile, he's every red-blooded girl's idea of a sexy terrorist leader!?!

OK, so he's responsible for the death of six thousand people in New York, but then love's a crazy thing?!?

Take me into your cave and show me your secret arsenal!?! Geddit!?! That's what I call Biological Phwoarfare!! (Geddit?!?)

The above paragraph has been deemed unhelpful by the Government's D-Notice Committee, and the rest of the column, including Glenda's Men of the Month feature naming Saddam Hussein, Chairman Arafat, and Sulaiman Abu Ghaith ("crazy name, completely crazy guy") as her Ramadan Romeos, has been censored.

Byeeee!!

Land of Hope and Glory

(Schools' version approved by HM Government)

Oh we do like Muslims
We like them very much
How can we ever tell them
That they really are such
Wonderful people truly
Warm and caring and nice
With their mosques and
                    their mullahs
And their curry and rice.

(To be sung to original Elgar tune)

"And what would you like to be when you blow up?"

THAT PRINCE CHARLES NEW-LOOK HOSPITAL
What You Will See

Karmic Mud Healing Department ➡

⬅ **Tantric Ear Nose and Throat Clinic**

Multi-Faith Accident & Emergency ➡

⬅ **Organic Mortuary**

Japanese Hot-Stone Healing Centre ➡

⬅ **Sort of Feeling Better Thingie Ward**

Way Out Man ➡

"It's harsh reality TV"

HITLER WAS 'A NAZI'
Shock New Claim

by Our History Staff **Gay Search**

A NEW book about the life of Adolf Hitler has produced compelling new evidence that the former Führer was in fact a Nazi.

Historians have always believed that Hitler was just an ordinary homosexual who liked painting and dressing up in uniforms.

Now in his shocking new biography of the German leader, author Dr Münnigrübber reveals that Hitler was in fact a member of a far-right organisation bent on world domination.

Nowt So Queer As Volk

"He liked hanging around with other fascists wearing jackboots and invading Poland," says the controversial historian. "What more proof do you need? My book offers definite proof that any old rubbish about Hitler gets lots of publicity and huge pieces in the Telegraph."

Starting tomorrow: 'Did Hitler Have A Secret Moustache?'

What You Missed

GREAT QUEENS OF BRITAIN

No. 94:
Queen David of Starkey

Presented by Simon Schama

(Tudor-style music on virginals)

Schama *(on battlements of mediaeval-type castle)*: It was not far from here that, in the year 2001, the middle-aged David Starkey launched his second crusade to become more famous than me.

(Re-enactment of two historians in armour preparing to joust in TV studio)

Schama: David had scored an enormous triumph with his "Elizabeth". It had soared to the top of the ratings, and the book had featured briefly in the best-seller list.

(Shot of Schama gently fingering priceless manuscript in British Museum)

Schama: But would its successor, "The Eight Wives of Henry The Sixth" *(surely you mean "The Six Wives of Salman Rushdie"? Ed.)* be any good?

(Actor dressed as Queen David walks round Hampton Court Maze, accompanied by Tudor-style lute music. Cut to Starkey kneeling in gothic-style chapel, praying that his series would be successful)

Schama: But, tragically, it was not to be. The people of England looked fondly back to the good old days of the year 2000, when they had feasted on the far superior series "A History of Britain" by myself.

(Mass crowd scene involving three TV extras in Tudor-style doublets and hose, running across field with M25 visible in background)

Crowd: Down with the Old Queen! Long live King Schama.

(Cut to Queen David being beheaded on Tower Hill by Channel Four executive)

Executioner: You're for the chop.

*"Actually, I'm **militant** C of E"*

Exclusive Serialisation Of The Spy Book Of The Millennium

MONEYRAKER
BY JAMES BOND

Chapter 94

"MR BOND. So good of you to drop in."

Bond struggled against the steel wire pinning him to the chair in the control centre of Ernst Blofeld's underwater mountain lair.

"You disappoint me, Mr Bond. And now you will suffer a slow and painful death," continued Blofeld, laughing sinisterly.

"What have you got in mind?" spat Bond. "The rotating saw? The tank full of piranha fish? The laser gun directed at my testicles?"

Blofeld stroked his white cat and laughed again.

"Oh no, Mr Bond. I have something worse in mind. I am going to read you extracts from Stella Rimington's memoirs."

"You bastard," whimpered Bond as Blofeld produced a copy of the Guardian from behind his back and cleared his throat.

"The day I ordered more paper clips..."

Tomorrow: *How Bond escaped, skiied down a mountain, jumped on a helicopter, parachuted off a dam and abseiled into the offices of Hutchinson in order to flog the publishers his memoirs.*

Exclusive To Private Eye – The Boris Johnson Diaries

Chapter One

CRIKEY! I'm for it! I've sold my diaries to the Times and the rotters have put my picture all over the front page! And I'm meant to work for the Telegraph! Ooo-err!

Chapter Two

THE cheque has arrived! Yarooo! Straight down to the tuckshop for lashings of ginger pop and sticky buns!

Chapter Three

UH-OH! My boss Charles is in a terrific bate! Blimey! Even my friend Lord Black is fuming with yours truly! Better put a copy of my book down my trousers!!

Chapter Four

OUCH!! Howl!! Whimper!! I've had a thrashing from the beak. And my book was too thin to help! Cripes!

Chapter Five

BOO hoo hoo! I'm going to be sacked! What will I do? I'll have to be an MP, I suppose. Thinks: crikey! That's no fun.

TOMORROW: Boris becomes leader of the Conservative Party *(Some mistake surely?)*

School news

St Cakes

Celebrity Term begins today. There are 1,412 children of celebrities in the school. B. Beckham (Spice's) is Senior Celeb. Ms M. Winslet (Titanic's) is Head Toddler. O.K. Magazine (Desmond's) is Keeper of the Photos. The Rev. M. Barrymore has had to retire, following a swimming accident, and will be replaced as Chaplin by Father Max Clifford. Mr and Mrs Neil Hamilton have joined the domestic staff as matron and odd-job man. Catwalks will be on Nov. 14. A performance of *The Graduate* will take place in the Groucho Theatre (auditions for mothers of children currently in the school will be on Oct. 12. Apply to C. Macintosh, head of drama). The O.C. Dinner (guest of honour Nigella Lawson O.C.) will be at Paparazzi's, on Dec. 24 (for tickets, apply Richard Branson, Dunvirgin, Carey Street). Raps will be on Dec 12.

THAT AFGHANISTAN STRIKE

BEFORE

AFTER

1 **Chemical Warfare Centre**
2 **Nuclear Missile Silo Disguised As Rock**
3 **Telecommunications Centre Camouflaged As Tree**
4 **Anthrax Production Facility (Camel Dung)**
5 **Terrorist Barracks (To Hold Up To 2000 Fully-Trained Mass-Murderers)**
6 **Barber's Shop (Closed By Order Of Taliban)**
7 **Prob. Bin Laden In Tent**

Nothing

PARLIAMENTARY DEBATES

(Han-z-z-z-ard)

That Amazing Iain Duncan Smith Commons Debut In Full

3.17 pm. The President's Question Time

Iain Duncan Smith (Wheen North, Con): May I ask the Prime Minister who I am?

President Blair: I would like to congratulate the Rt. Hon. Gentleman on his recent election as leader of the Conservative Party. *(Consults folder of jokes, prepared by A. Campbell.)* I won't say "Leader of the Opposition", because there isn't any!

(Sycophantic laughter from Labour benches)

Duncan Stoat: I say, I don't think that's very funny, especially since I've been jolly supportive over the war. I've been a very good opposition – I've agreed with everything you've said.

Blair: You're meant to ask a question, you know. How about "Does the Prime Minister agree that he's doing a superb job in defending freedom and democracy?"

Patsy Jacket (Consignia, New Lab): Hang on, that's the question I was going to ask.

Blair: Sorry, Patsy, you can ask me another one, like "Does the Prime Minister agree that he has done a marvellous job in bringing peace not only to Northern Ireland but to the whole world?"

Jacket: OK, Tony, that'll be great. Thank you!

Tam O'Shanter (Dalyell, Old Lab): Could the Prime Minister explain why, as a lifelong opponent of cluster bombs, he is now dropping them on the heads of innocent Afghan women and children?

Hilary Strongarm (Whiplash, New Lab): How dare you ask Sir Winstony that sort of question! You're worse than the Nazis, you Quisling scum. I know where you live!

(Labour cheers and cries of "String up the Old Etonian bastard!")

Paul Newbloke (Newsbury, Newish Lab): Since we're meant to be fighting this war in the name of democracy, do you think we could have a vote?

(Labour uproar, cries of "Resign!", "Judas!", "Hitler!", "Osama Bin Marsden!" etc etc)

"Congratulations, it's a bomb!"

12

Friday, November 2, 2001

OUR BRAVE LADS GO IN!

by Our Man In Peshawar
MICHAEL BURQA

THE FIRST British troops have been involved in the fighting in the war against terrorism.

A small unit of highly-trained British muslims were dropped behind the lines in Kabul and immediately proceeded to engage with the enemy.

Tragically, they gave their lives for their country (Afghanistan) and were buried with full military honours by the Taliban.

Hang On – Is This Right?

As a small detachment of soldiers fired rifles at British aircraft and sang "Allah, Don't Save The Queen" a Taliban General said, "We are grateful to Britain for its support in this war against the great Satan." *(Shurely shome mishtake? Ed.)*

OUR BRAVE LADS DON'T GO IN

PLUCKY England cricketers bravely announced last night that they were too scared to go to India. "Have you seen their bowlers?" said one. "That Kumble bloke *(cont. p. 94)*

WHERE'S OZZY?

Osama bin Laden is hiding somewhere in this jolly scene. Can YOU find him without turning the whole area into a smouldering pile of ash?

BUSH DECLARES WAR ON TOURISM

by Our Washington Staff **Ann Thrax** and **Spore Vidal**

President Bush last night announced an all–out war on international tourism.

"We are well on the way," he said, "to wiping tourism off the face of the globe."

"These people can run, but they can't fly," said the President.

"We will not only put an end to tourists. We will end those organisations which support them – the international network of airlines, travel agents, hotel chains, and so on.

"And that includes all those folks who sell postcards of the Leaning Tower of Eiffel, and the Bridge Over The River Sighs."

At this point Mr Bush was interrupted by Secretary Colin Powell, who issued a clarification. "When the President used the word tourist instead of terrorist, he did not of course mean to offend the millions of bona fide terrorists who are going peacefully round the world murdering people."

13

Daily Mail

FRIDAY, NOVEMBER 2, 2001

Newspaper of the Year

NEW ANTHRAX THREAT TO HOUSE PRICES

By Our Scare Staff
Anne Thrax

HOUSE prices are in free fall, as the anthrax terror sweeps Britain, the Mail can reveal.

Millions of young couples are selling up and emigrating to safer regions of the world, such as Washington, New York and Afghanistan – leading to a catastrophic slump in property values all over the south-east of England.

Filthy Dacre

A typical 3-bedroom family home in Finchley, which was last week worth £1 million, is today worth a mere £34, say estate agents Shyster and Cheatham, and "even then they will have problems finding a buyer".

But house prices are only one of the rising avalanche of problems unleashed in the wake of the deadly anthrax scare.

Death By Mail

Investment analysts of the Daily Mail City Staff estimate that millions of Britain's pension holders are facing bankruptcy and lengthy gaol sentences when they reach 65, rather than the £100,000-a-year tax–free retirement to the Costa Brava that they have been saving for over decades of hard work.

The average Daily Mail reader contributing £50 a month to his or her with-profit nest-egg will now be lucky to receive 35p a week as a pension, and will be forced to beg in the streets or sell crack cocaine outside the gates of their local primary school in order to survive.

As the number of anthrax cases in Britain yesterday soared to zero, there are growing fears that *(cont. p.94)*

■ EARL SPENCER, brother of the Prince of Wales's ex-wife, Lady Diana Cooper, the ex-husband of the supermodel Victoria Beckham, is to marry again I can reveal. His bride-to-be is none other than Sir Clement Freud,

Nigel Dumpster's Diary

Wedding of the Century

youngest daughter of famed psychiatrist and dog-food lover Sigmund Freud, the ex-husband of Elizabeth Murdoch, daughter of Sir Rupert Allason and Dame Iris Murdoch, the Press Baron and disgraced Tory MP. The Earl's fiancée was formerly married to the ex-husband of film star Dame Margaret Lockwood and his previous girlfriends include cartoonist Silly-Ann Legover and Erotic Review editor Dame Rowenta Pelling. The Earl will be given away by his brother-in-law PR man Matthew Freud who is recently divorced from famous criminal and old Etonian Sir Darius Guppy whose father was a well-known fun-loving tropical fish I need a drink *(You're fired. Ed.)*

14

Radio 3 Highlights

● WAS HANDEL GAY?
<u>You</u> decide!
10 Tell-tale Signs That Could Help You Make Up Your Mind.

1. He was unmarried.

2. Wore a wig.

3. Lived near Soho.

4. Liked playing with his organ.

5. Looked like Elton John.

6. Was "Musical".

7. Wore stockings and high heels.

8. Wrote music admired by many members of the gay community.

9. ...er...

10. ...he must have been.

■ **What's more, just look at these top Handel's 'homo' hits.**
- ● *The Hallosailor Chorus*
- ● *The Entrance of the Old Queen of Sheba*
- ● *Gaydok the Priest*
- ● Plus millions more.

Just phone the Radio 3 "Was Handel Gay Line" and say why you're switching to Classic FM.

That Amazing Barrymore TV Interview In Full

Martin Bashir: Your Highness, it is very good of you to speak to the nation at this very difficult time for you.

Princess Michael of Barrymore: Indeed it is.

Martin Bashir: Can you tell us your feelings about the sad events that have overtaken you in recent days?

Princess Michael: It is a terrible tragedy that I am no longer on television. I have to take the blame for that and the death of my career is something I'm going to have to live with for the rest of my life.

Martin Bashir: Your Majesty, with your permission, may I turn now to the difficult subject of your private life?

Princess Michael: I've never really loved anyone. Except myself. Oh, and the police for letting me off. I love them obviously.

Martin Bashir: How do you see your role in the future of the nation, Ma'am?

Princess Michael: I want to put this all behind me and become the Queen of Television, the People's Pooftah.

Martin Bashir: And finally – is there anything else you would like to say to me?

Princess Michael: Would you like to come back to my place for a drink?

Martin Bashir: Er... er...

Sir Trevor Barbados: And that concludes our look at the World At War tonight.

TODAY'S TV CHOICE

■ **Couples Shagging In Ibiza** Channel 4 lifestyle show presented by Davina McStoat 9.00pm.

■ **Sex Vampires Rampage** Channel 5 adult film 1.45pm.

■ **Live Swearing From Uttoxeter** Channel 4 sport with Paul Ross.

■ **Whose Knob Is It Anyway?** BBC1 9.00pm. Blue quiz show hosted by Rory McBeard and Jonathan Dross. (A Toppo Thompson Production.)

■ **The Bonking Chef** BBC2. Thai cuisine for ladyboys, served up by she-male celebrity chef Jamie Nigella.

■ **Why Mary Whitehouse Was Wrong** Documentary, Channel 4. Lily Savage reassesses the reputation of the late TV clean-up campaigner *(That's enough TV. Ed.)*

BARRYMORE CLEARED

It was a bum rap

COFFEE
o BURN HANDS
→ RUIN SHOES

RGJ

THIS WEEK

JILLY COOPER

Are you a spoon person?

Oh yes, I think spoons are really sexy! I mean, they're really round and curvy – lovely to cup in the palm of your hand – mmmmm!

What's your favourite sort of spoon?

Oh, no doubt about it, a great, big, naughty soup spoon, to plunge into a lovely, thick, steamy cockaleekie. I'd go anywhere for a nice thick cockaleekie! Oh, I am jolly naughty, aren't I?

Have you written much about spoons in your books?

I certainly have! One of my favourite bits in one of my early novels, *Chef*, describes how the hero, an absolutely gorgeous young Old Etonian running a little bistro in the Cotswolds, takes a big wooden spoon and spanks one of his waitresses, Lucinda Rumpington-Pumpington, because she's spilt a great bowl of cockaleekie all over the Earl of Lymeswold's new pin-stripe trousers. One thing leads to another, as you can imagine, and it's not long before they're at it like knives. Or spoons, I suppose!

Some people say you've got spoons on the brain?

No, it's sex. But I love dogs as well, don't you? I wept absolutely buckets of tears when we had to put down Parker-Bowles, our 18-year-old labrador. Dogs never let you down, do they? That's what's so marvellous about them.

Can we get back to spoons please. Has anything amusing ever happened to you in connection with a spoon?

Oh yes, heaps of things.

You're supposed to say 'no'.

Am I? Gosh, sorry!

NEXT WEEK: The Bishop of Oxford — *"Me And My Thermos".*

POETRY CORNER

In Memoriam
Stratford Johns,
television actor

So. Farewell then
Stratford Johns.

Better known as
Inspector Barlow
Of Z Cars.
And Softly Softly.

There was you,
Frank Windsor
And the one
From Northern
Ireland.

Altogether now, Da-da-da
De-dum-dum-dum-dum
Da-da-da
De-dum-dum-dum.
That was the theme tune
That made you
Famous.

E.J. Thribb (17½)

In Memoriam
Ken Aston *(The football*
referee who introduced red
and yellow cards)

So. Farewell
Then.
Ken Aston.
Referee
And soccer
Inventor.

Now you
Have been
Shown the red
Card and must
Leave the field.

E.J. Thribb (17½)

In Memoriam
David Astor, owner of the
Observer Newspaper

So. Farewell
Then.
David Astor.

Famous owner
Of the Observer.

Your death
Made headlines.

But only
In the
Observer.

E.J. Thribb (17½)

16

Scenes You Seldom See

*"Have you got some more leaflets I can
give to my friends?"*

"Thank you – I'll take six"

"That was lovely – would you play it again?"

In Memoriam
Joe "Spud" Murphy, Irish
inventor of the cheese-
and-onion flavoured crisp

So. Farewell
Then.
Joe "Spud"
Murphy.
You invented the legendary
Cheese-and-onion
Flavoured crisp.

"Oi'll have a pint of
Guinness
And a packet of those new
Cheese-and-onion flavoured
Crisps, please, sor."

That was the catchphrase
You taught to a whole
Generation
Of crisp eaters.

Since then, many other
Combinations of flavours
Have been
Introduced.
But yours remains
The most tasty.

E.J. Thribb (17½)
E.J. Thribb's latest verse-drama
Salt In A Blue Bag is
available on his website
www.sofarewellthen.com

In Memoriam Cranks,
the health food shop

So. Farewell
Then
Cranks.

"Lentil soup?"

That was your
Catchphrase.

Unfortunately your
Profits
Were not so
Healthy.

E.J. Thribb
(17½ calories)

In Memoriam
Prof. Stanley Unwin,
Master of Gobbledygook

Farewellylode. So. Thenfull
Stanwin Unleymold.

Poppetyclogs
Toesyturnyup.

Deep joy
Or rather
Sadlymost.

E.J. Thribbledygook (½17)

In Memoriam
Barry Foster,
TV's Van Der Valk

So. Farewell then
Barry Foster.

You were known to
Millions as
Dutch detective
Inspector Van Der Valk.

Da-da-da-da
Dadada
Da-da-da-da-da-da.

That was your
Theme tune.

Keith points out
That you were the second
Famous TV detective
To die
Within a month.

The other being
Stratford Johns
Or Inspector Barlow
Of Z-Cars fame.

For those who missed
My last poem
His theme tune was
Da-da-da
De-dum-dum-dum-dum etc.

Who will be the next
To go?

It is a job for a
Detective.

P.C. Thribb (49½)

In Memoriam
Kenneth Wolstenholme,
Football Commentator

So. Farewell
Then
Kenneth Wolstenholme.

Famous commentator
On the World Cup 1966.
The greatest moment
In the entire history
Of sport.

Those 14 words you said
Have passed into
Legend.

Unfortunately I
Cannot remember
Them all.
But the last ones were
"They think it's all over.
It is now."

It would be a fitting epitaph
To put on your
Gravestone.

E.J. Thribb (4-2)

Scenes You Seldom See

"Should we turn it down a bit?"

"Do you know of any litter bins around here?"

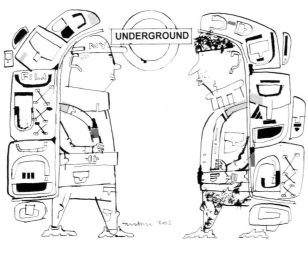

*"Better take off our packs in case they
injure someone..."*

In Memoriam
Rosemary Brown,
Medium to the Great
Composers

So. Farewell
Then.
Rosemary Brown.

You are the
Famous Balham
Housewife
Who wrote down
Music dictated
To her
By Bach, Beethoven,
Liszt and
Many others.

You also saw
Bertrand
Russell in the
Supermarket.

I have just
Seen you in
My bedroom
Telling me
To write this
Poem.

E.J. Thribb (17½)

In Memoriam
Dean Riesner,
Screenwriter

So. Farewell
Then
"Dinky" Dean Riesner.

No-one had
Ever heard of
You.

But you wrote
The immortal
Lines

"Do you feel lucky?
Well do you.
Punk?"

And "Go ahead
Make my day".

You always
Made mine

When I saw
Clint deliver
Your catchphrases.

E.J. "Dirty" Thribb,
(17½ Precinct)

•••• Gnome Special ••••
Frost Commemorative Mug Offer

A great British invention takes to the air again! New Yorkers, headed by their popular Mayor Giuliani, thronged JFK airport to welcome the most legendary British export of them all, Sir David Frost, now resuming his four-times weekly flights across the Atlantic, after a year when he has been tragically grounded. World-famous artist Sir Ralph Stoddy, Fellow of the Royal Society of Commemorative Ceramic Mug Designers and Engravers, captures the unique moment when this much-loved symbol of all that is best in modern Britain boards his favourite aeroplane for its historic flight.

A limited edition of 5 million "Frost-on-Concorde" mugs are available now, for only £1.95 each (including VAT, p&p).

Each of these priceless heritage items will be treasured for generations to come. Not only will they enhance the beauty of your home, they will be a wonderful investment for you, your children, your children's children and their live-in partners.

WARNING

The value of commemorative mugs may go down as well as up. Commemorative mug values are monitored by Offmug, the regulatory body responsible for supervision of the commemorative mug industry.

Send money now to Gnome Frost Mug Offer, Unit 16B, The Trading Estate, Chorleywood NBG 123

"I sometimes think these no-frills airlines go too far"

CHAMPAGNE FLIES AS CONCORDE FLOWS IN
by Lunchtime O'Booze

FANTASTIC! That wash the word that wash on the lipsh of every journalisht (writes Bill Deedesh) as the corks lifted gracefully off the bottlesh of champagne and flew across the cabin of Concorde at shupershonic shpeed.

There ish no doubt that the bringing of Concorde back into shervice after a year hash been the perfect reminder to our American friendsh that British journalists are the drunkesht in the world.

As we touched down in wherever it was, our heartsh went out to all thoshe who'd laid on this terrific shpree!

On Other Pages

CITY NEWS: British Airways Faces Bankruptcy Following £500 Million Concorde Drinks Bill

MIRROR EDITOR BRAVELY GOES ON FREEBIE WITH CELEBRITIES

BLUNKETT ARRESTED UNDER NEW TERRORIST LAW

by **Phil Jails**

A SINISTER-looking blind man with a beard was arrested yesterday near the House of Commons under the new Detention of Dodgy-Looking Bearded Men Act (2001).

Under the new act, any dodgy-looking bearded men can be detained at Her Majesty's Pleasure without trial, charge or evidence. Only a beard is needed by the police as proof that the man in question is a danger to civilised values, such as freedom to walk around without being arrested.

BLUNKETT COVERAGE

David Blunkett last night was delighted at his arrest.

"This is a triumph for justice," he said. "It shows that none of us is safe under my new regulations."

CAKES' HEAD LASHES OUT AT 'LEAGUE TABLE FARCE'

by Educational Staff **Conrad Blackboard**

THE HEADMASTER of the prestigious independent school St Cakes (Motto: 'Who Pays Gets In') hit out yesterday at the latest academic league tables which show his school to be the bottom of the list for the fourth year running.

Said Mr Kipling, "These tables give no indication of the overall quality of a school. They just centre on things like education and ignore all the other things that a school is doing, like collecting fees and renting out the facilities for conferences in the holidays."

He continued, "If you would like to know more about our leisure facilities, which now include an 18-hole golf course, you can visit our website at www.stcakes.co.uk where full details are available."

League Tables In Full pages 12-58

MIDLANDS		GCSE PASS RATE
375	St Botolphs, Handsworth Ind. RC Grant-maintained (425 pupils)	7%
376	Bogstandard Comprehensive, Solihull Comp. Co-ed (37,304 pupils)	6%
377	The Taliban School For Girls, Aston Ind. Islamic (0 pupils)	3%
378	St Cakes School (off the M73) Ind. Co-ed (743 pupils)	0%

"Oh no – I've been tracked down by Friendsreunited"

Who's In The Running For Scotland's Top Job?

The Eye's Cut-Out-And-Keep Guide

1. JENNY MCPENNY *(MSP for Glen Isskinnoch)*, 38, high-flying woman you have never heard of who has said she doesn't want the job.

2. Hugh McHee *(MSP for Dinnaeken)*, 57, high-flying Scotsman from the lowlands about whom very little is known.

3. Tony McCrony *(MSP for Fettes)*, 63, high-flying friend of Mr Blair who will probably get the job.

4. Gordon McBrownnose *(MSP for Ben Doon)*, 47, high-flying chief of the clan McBrownnose. Was at school with Gordon Brown so he may get the job if McCrony doesn't.

5. Rory McSleaze *(MSP for Dunfiddlin)*, 57, high-flying crook who is in prison for embezzlement, which may be a handicap to his ambitions of becoming Scotland's First Minister.

6. Osama McBin Laden *(MSP for Fingal's Cave)*, 94, high-flying outside candidate who lives somewhere in the Hebrides.

(That's enough candidates. Ed.)

SCOTTISH POLITICIAN ADMITS 'NOT HAVING AFFAIR'

by Our Scottish Staff **Brillo McPad**

MR DOUGLAS McClean, MSP, has told a specially called news conference that he has never had an affair with a member of the party nor fiddled his expenses.

Sitting beside his stony-faced wife, Mrs Squeaky McClean, the contrite Labour member for the Isles of Muck and Lairgover, apologised for letting down the party.

"I realise that this is not the conduct that people expect of a Scottish politician in this day and age.

"I shall be resigning forthwith and I shall leave the political field clear for those more worthy of high office."

Mr McLegover (MSP) now becomes First Minister of Scotland.

"Oh dear... a burglary... not much we can do... no"

POLICE VAPID RESPONSE UNIT

health

Bin Laden – Has He Got Cancer?

By Our Medical Correspondent **Dr Thomas Utterfraud**

FROM the grainy pictures on Al-Jezira television, it is quite clear that Osama bin Laden has only three weeks to live. The first clue is his beard, which has lost its sheen. This is symptomatic of severe renal failure. The second clue is the disturbing colour of his skin which, even in black-and-white, is looking worryingly yellow, a clear sign of Hepatitis B, brought on by living in damp caves and having to survive on a diet of American food parcels. The final clue is a piece in the Telegraph saying that last June he was in hospital in Dubai where he was diagnosed as having liver problems.

TOMORROW: Dr Utterfraud asks "Am I Psychotic? You Decide"

Simpson of Kabul

THE heroic deeds of Simpson of Kabul are known to every schoolboy in the land and have now passed into legend. Armed only with a microphone and dressed up as an Afghan woman, Simpson marched into Kabul and single-handedly captured the Taliban fortress without a shot being fired. According to the only eye witness (Jo Simpson), at the sight of the distinguished silver-haired Englishman, the entire Taliban army turned tail and ran.

Some left their weapons lying on the ground, some left meals half-eaten and opium pipes half-smoked. Others did not even have time to shave off their beards. They simply fled in blind terror at the sight of the man known only as The BBC's Global Editor.

Simpson's first words on entering the liberated city will be remembered as long as history is taught in British schools. "1, 2, 3... Testing, testing... Is this bloody camera working?"

© The Boys' Own Book of Bogus Adventures

The Sun

IS OZZIE GAY?
TEN TELL-TALE SIGNS THAT PROVE BIN LADEN IS A POOF

1 **Wears a dress**
2 **Long beard**
3 **Funny eyes**
4 **Hangs around with other men in caves**
5 **Supports the Talibum**
6 **Arse-nal fan**
7 **Big fan of Judy Garland**

8 **Has four wives and 45 children**
9 **Er...**
10 **Well, he's got to be, hasn't he?**
11 **No offence to the gay community**
12 **That's it**

APOLOGY
The Conduct Of The War

IN COMMON with all other newspapers employing military experts, we may in recent weeks have inadvertently given the impression that the Taliban military forces were comprised of fanatical, battle-hardened combat troops whose warrior ancestry and fighting prowess would ensure that the war against them would be long, bloody and ultimately unsuccessful. Headlines such as "Bombing Doesn't Work", "Why We Must Surrender Now" and "This War Is Nothing But Hot Blair" may have reinforced this misapprehension amongst our readers.

We now accept that far from being a dangerous army of suicidal maniacs, the Taliban are in fact an ill-disciplined, disorganised, gutless rabble, who scarper at the first sound of gunfire and then switch sides to try and save themselves.

Talking of which, we would like to congratulate the Prime Minister on his courageous handling of the war and have run a number of pieces in today's paper with headlines reflecting our consistent support for his conduct of a complex military situation, viz "Bombs Wahay!", "Why They Must Surrender Now" and "Yes! Winstony Blair Has Won The War".

We would like to apologise for any confusion caused by our earlier coverage.

© *All newspapers.*

Exclusive To All Papers
SHOULD TONY BLAIR GET INVOLVED IN POLITICS?

THERE was much disquiet in political circles yesterday after Tony Blair, the husband of the first lady Cherie Blair, made a speech where he made a number of comments about the situation in Afghanistan.

"While we all agree that Tony is lovely to look at and that he always makes an effort to support Cherie in her work," said one political observer, "he really isn't qualified to speak on such complex and difficult matters, in the manner that a QC such as Cherie could.

"In future, Tony would be better advised to leave such complex world matters to his vastly more intelligent wife and just get on with whatever it is that he does."

BLAIR'S PLAN FOR THE NEW AFGHANISTAN PARLIAMENT

1. A new reformed House of Warlords to be selected by an independent commission.

2. The independent commission to be comprised of former warlords appointed by an independent select committee.

3. The independent select committee to consist of senior warlords appointed directly by T. Blair (King).

4. That's enough. Ed.

Plan devised by the Head of the Prime Minister's Delivery Unit, the Chief Dalek Lord Birt of Suit.

THE DAILY TELEGRAPH   Friday, November 2, 2001

Letters to the Editor

Dying with Dignity

SIR – Like many of your readers, I have been deeply touched by the story of the unfortunate woman whose husband has for years been trying to assist her to die with dignity. Who amongst us I wonder, will not have entertained similar thoughts about their lady wife? Yet now the law has again cruelly denied the husband the right to administer a peaceful end to the years of misery they have shared together.

In your admirable campaign to re-establish Britain as a "free country", perhaps you should add the right of a husband to kill my wife with dignity to those you have already espoused, namely the right to watch adult videos on the internet and to smoke the occasional spliff in the privacy of one's own drawing room.

I remain, sir, your befuddled servant,
Sir H. Gussett
Euthanasia Cottage, Boycott St. Rosie, Dorset

"Oh, your mother rang – your father's died"

THE SUNDAY TIMES ● November 16, 2001

The End Of Celebrity

by A.A. Homestart

IT'S OFFICIAL! The cult of celebrity is over. In the wake of the events of the 11th September, there is no longer any public appetite for personality-based trivia about figures in the media. We have moved on from this childish obsession with fame and its trappings to a more responsible and sobre awareness of the gravity of real life.

INSIDE

❏ Big pictures of the celebrities we are no longer obsessed with **page 2**

❏ Interviews with Madonna, Britney and Kylie about their reaction to the end of celebrity **page 3**

❏ J.K. Rowling buys some knickers **pages 4-94**

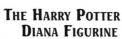

Heirs and Graces

by Dame Sylvie Krin

THE STORY SO FAR: The beautiful flower of the Orient, Wendy Deng, has married billionaire media mogul Rupert Murdoch. Now she is about to present him with another heir...

"**P**USH! Harder! Come on, you can do it! Just one more push! You're nearly there!" Rupert tried desperately to raise his ageing frame an inch from the floor, under the stern gaze of his personal trainer, the former world Kung Fu Champion Mr Givima Kikin.

The octogenarian press baron felt the sweat forming on his wrinkled brow as he struggled to obey Mr Kikin's commands.

"Ten more press-ups, now, or Miss Wendy say you have no breakfast, fat guy!"

"Jeez! Give us a break, ya yellow bastard," panted the owner of the Times of London and 417 other international titles. "I'm fair pooped!"

He collapsed onto the exercise mat in the purpose-built gymnasium on the 37th floor of his Manhattan love-nest.

"I feel as knackered as a wallaby's donger in the mating season," he wheezed and he was saved from further exertion by the urgent ringing of his mobile phone with its personalised ring tone of Rolf Harris's "Two Little Boys". The screen flashed up

the number of the Graydon Carter Maternity Clinic in fashionable downtown Long Island.

"Mr Murdoch?" purred the silken voice of Dr Hackenbush, New York's leading gynaecologist. "I think you should come over at once."

"**T**HEY told me to come over at once," Rupert explained to the pretty young receptionist who greeted him at the clinic's welcome area.

"You must be the proud grandfather," she beamed, extending a cordial hand. "You haven't seen the father anywhere, have you? We did ring, but we haven't seen him."

Thrusting her aside with his huge bouquet of purple magnesias mixed with yellow nigellas, which his chauffeur had purchased at the service station on the way over, the world's most powerful press magnate strode purposefully towards the lift.

"Take me to the maternity ward!" he snapped at the bell-boy, pressing a ten cent coin into the black youth's open palm.

"And don't spend it all at once," he added. "I worked bloody hard for that."

"Thank you, Sah," came back the reply from the grateful lift attendant. "You must be the proud grandfather."

The lift door opened and he was met by the matron, a buxom middle-aged hispanic

lady in a starched uniform and an identity badge which stated 'Sister Cavaleria Rusticana – sponsored by McDonald's'.

"Congratulaziones, señor! You are the happy grandfather, no?"

"No, I am *bloody* not!" yelled the indignant entrepreneur. "Do I look like a bloody chinaman?" The matron shrugged. "Just bring the flowers anyway. I get you a nice glass of water and find you somewhere to sit until the husband comes."

Rupert's eyes bulged with rage and his walnut-veined cheeks suffused with anger.

"I am the bloody husband! If anyone else calls me the grandfather again, I'll buy this clinic and close it down!"

"**L**UPERT! So good to see you?" The third Mrs Murdoch raised her head from the pillow. In her arms she cradled the tiny helpless heir to the Murdoch dynasty. "She's a great little Sheila and no mistake," Rupert announced proudly as he gazed tenderly into the baby's eyes. "She's only a little thing. How much was she? About six pounds?"

"No," his wife replied knowingly, as a smile played across her perfectly formed cherry blossom lips. "More like six billion!"

As she spoke, the matron pulled back the blind and golden sunlight filled the room with its rich splendour. *(To be continued)*

KING GOES TO PRISON

Hey! Wow! I'm Number One-Three-Seven-Six-Nine-Five!

"I'm sorry – we can take your mother's clothes, but not her"

Notes & Queries

QUESTION: Can anyone explain why so many places in the country are called "Parkway" – eg, Didcot Parkway, Tiverton Parkway, etc?

☐ THE name "Parkway" derives from the old Norse word "Parkvauga", originally meaning "a clearing in the forest", where travellers could leave their wagons while they engaged in marauding expeditions to the city of Londinium.

Question: Who invented the pizza?

☐ THE first-ever recorded pizza was served, surprisingly, in London in 1762, by an Italian immigrant Giovanni Battista Pizza. Even more surprisingly, it bore little resemblance to the pizza we know today, consisting as it did of two pieces of bread enclosing a slice of ham or cheese.

Question: Why can we see through glass?

☐ GLASS is made from a compound of silicates, hydrogen chloride and mono-sodium glutamate. When these are heated to a temperature of 800 degrees celsius, the dense particulate matter is dissolved, leaving only a thin, brittle film, which is transparent.

Answers, please, to the following: a) Is it true that ping-pong was invented by Cistercian monks in the 12th century? b) Can fish drown? c) Is Peter Jay still alive?

POLLY FILLER

An open letter to Kate Winslet

DEAR KATE – Happy Christmas to you and little Mia! If ever there was a mother and child who deserve our sympathy at Christmas, it's you! Because, guess what, all the men who run the media have decided to brand you a slapper, Kate, just because you dumped your boring husband and went off with someone more famous.

Well, excuse me, isn't that what we women have been fighting for for the past 100 years? The right to choose someone more interesting?

Kate – I salute you. You are a wonderful role model for working women everywhere, a feminist icon for the twenty-first century, and you are looking really thin and blonde as well. What more could one ask?

Let's have no tears shed for dull Jim looking after the baby, changing the nappies and staying up all night. Welcome to motherhood, Jim! No, let's hear it for the svelte, in control, up-front, sassy überchick who knows exactly what she wants and how to get it – ie, an alpha male with money, fame, Oscars and the power to cast you in films. Clever girl, Katie!

SO, that's a message to all you men, including you, the useless Simon, as you sit watching sumo hamsters from Okinawa on the Granada Sad Sport Channel whilst the nanny Kirsten complains about taking Charlie to see Harry Potter for the seventh time.

Either get successful, rich and famous or start checking out the M&S "Singles" range of meals for one. Because, for low achievers like you, Dump City is only just around the corner.

Good luck Kate, and if Sam's next movie is a bummer, you know what to do. The women of Britain are right behind you.

Happy Christmas, sister!

Polly

"His last words were… 'Right from today, I'm going to start going to the gym'"

23

NEW ERA DAWNS AS MILLIONS QUEUE FOR EUROS

by Our Entire Staff

MAKE NO MISTAKE. January 1 2002 will go down in history as the day when the world changed for ever.

It was the day the foaming Europhobes said would never happen.

Yet all over Europe, from Bruges to Berlin, from Kilkenny to Kathmandu, the story was the same.

Millions of ordinary herrs and fraus, señors and señoras, hommes and dames proved the dismal jimmies wrong as they queued for hours to get their hands on the currency that spells unity for ever on this once war-torn continent.

Fuehrer What A Scorcher

I spoke yesterday morning to a typical Belgian housewife, Mrs Ludmilla Maigret, 67, who was living proof that the launch of the euro has been a total, 100 percent triumph.

"Oh yes," she admitted, her eyes shining, as she proudly showed me the new coins in her purse.

"They told us that if we wanted to go to the supermarket we would have to use them. It's all beyond me."

Meanwhile, ten thousand miles away above the Arctic Circle, the Finnish inhabitants of the tiny Lapland settlement of Tapioca were busy celebrating the most exciting event which has ever happened in their country in their time-honoured fashion, by gulping down litres of their favourite local tipple, a fiery spirit distilled from pine cones and reindeer dung.

The only inhabitant of the town sober enough to give me a quote, 81-year-old Aarro Kentainan, told me, "This is a great day for us all. I now feel we are all one great big family, bound together by the fact that we have no idea what is going on."

C'est La Même Change

But as Europe danced and sang far into the night, there was universal criticism for the country that refused to join the party.

"It's always the same with you English," said Breton baguette salesman Gerard Depardieu. "You sit around on the sidelines, wondering whether to join in, just like you did in 1940."

"Run!... They have the advantage of height"

HOW EUROPE READ THE HISTORIC NEWS

LE FIGARO 1.1.02
BONJOUR A L'EURO!

La Repubblica 1.1.02
BUON GIORNO EURO!

BERLINER TAGEBLAT 1.1.02
GUTEN MORGEN EURO!

The Daily Hurleygraph 1.1.02
Liz's Baby – New Tests
by Charles Moore
pages 2-16

THE CURRENCIES WE SHALL NEVER SEE AGAIN
No. 94 The Tostado

THE TOSTADO is one of Europe's oldest currencies. It was introduced in 1238 by Moorish invaders, under Caliph Abdul the Wicked. It was abolished in 1326 when the throne was reclaimed by the Christian Emperor Don Alfonso XXIII, but revived again in 1936 by the Fascist dictator General Portillo Bastardar. Following the revolution, the Tostado went through several devaluations, so that today there are 4 million tostados to the pound.

Tomorrow: The Gromek

Fashion News *by Our Style Staff* **May Kova**

It's Sexy! It's Fun! It's the Euro!

THERE'S been nothing like it since Mary Quant invented the mini-skirt way back in the swinging Sixties.

Suddenly, all over Europe, there's only one fashion accessory which counts – one that says "You're Numero Uno" in the fast-moving world of where it's at. The message is – bin your mobile and chuck away last year's baseball hat.

The only thing that says "I'm 2002" and tells the world that you're a switched-on sex freak is that shiny new little coin a-jinglin' and a-janglin' in your pocket or your purse.

© W. Rees-Mogg 2002

WICKED *Whispers*

Our sensational new celebrity column that dishes the dirt on celebrities...

PSSST! WHICH red-top newspaper, whose editor's name sounds suspiciously like 'moron', has for over a year been running a column called 'Wicked Whispers', peddling second-rate anonymous celebrity tat...?

PSSST! WHICH pisspoor editor of a newspaper that rhymes with 'snail' is now publishing the exact same column and trying to pass it off to his readers as something new...?

PSSST! IF this certain pisspoor editor thought nobody would notice this, how psss-t must he have been?

PSSST! THAT'S enough 'Wicked Whispers'. Ed.

That Honorary Degree Citation in Full

SALUTAMUS GEORGIUM BESTUM QUONDAM EXPERTO LUDUM BALLOS PEDICULOS PRO MANCUNIUM UNIFICATUM SUB LEGENDARIUS MATTHEUS BUSBEIUS ET ATQUE PRO HIBERNIA NORDICA DRIBULO WIZARDICUM CUM MAGICIS PEDIBUS NOTUS AD MULTOS SCRIBULIS SOCCERENSIS QUAM E.I. ADDIBUS PER EXEMPLO MOSTOS MAGNIFICISSIMUS LUDOR IN HISTORIAM MUNDI SED IN VERITAS, EHEU! BIBULOSISSIMUS, INEBRIATUS SEMPER ET PISSARTICUS MAXIMUS QUI FREQUENTAVIT DISCOS CLUBOS NOCTOSQUE CUM MULTIBUS BLONDIBUS PNEUMATICUS IN MINIMIS SKIRTIBUS SED IAM DIXIT "SUM TEETOTALITER SOBERISSIMUS." SED, EHEU, NEMO CREDIT UNUM VERBUM SALUTAMUS BOTTOMIS UPPIS ET CHEERIOSUS!

Degree issued by the Bell's Whisky Polytechnic (formerly Queens University, Belfast)

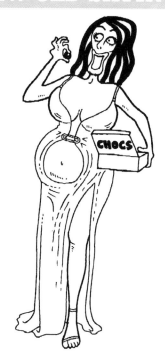

AUNTON Deane Council has performed a U-turn on cat pooh.

Somerset County Gazette

KEW GARDENS AND RICHMOND PARK. Large Victorian houses opposite Park and Kew Gardens, large self - contained bedsores, own modern kitchenette.

Richmond & Twickenham Times

Musical "Last Supper" Clock

Plays "Hallelujah Course" every hour.

Save 60%

7[.]**99**

Compare at $19.99

Advertisement, Phoenix, Arizona

THE HUNGRY NEED BREAD NOT BOMBS

From a Quaker poster

For a free pack on QUACKERS, their beliefs and their social concerns today, please fill in the form below

Observer

Illiteracy in children has risen, says study

ILITERACY among youngsters in 2001 is higher than before the First World War,

Argus (Brighton)

JACK-PUDDING JACK-STRAW CLOWN, BUFFOON WORTHLESS MAN

RSC programme note, Stratford

A SHRUB in a pot, worth £25 was stolen from Shrub End Road, Shrub End in Colchester.

Evening Gazette (Colchester)

A **LETTER** in last week's Doncaster Free Press, 'Concerned over new bus route' was attributed to Liberal Democrat campaigner Batty Hayes. The writer was in fact Barry Hayes.

Doncaster Free Press

Carpenter nailed in the head, but no brain damage

Daily Nation, SA

A **CRACKDOWN** on auto crime in East Cleveland is driving thieves into the long ars of the law.

East Cleveland Herald & Post

Katharine Viner £$^blah blah blah blah

ghgghg

Grauniad

English solicitors hope to inspire Ugandan ethics

Law Society Gazette

One woman and her dog: Clarissa Dickson Wright at Chatsworth House in Derbyshire (BBC2, 4.20 pm)

Daily Telegraph

Accordingly, the responsibility of criminal defence lawyers is very specific and specialised—they must take all possible steps to raise a reasonable doubt about the client's innocence.

New Law Journal

7.30 The Good Life A debate on the political future of Northern Ireland.

Sun TV guide

LEGAL SECRETARY required for bust solicitors in Birkenhead,

Daily Post

It was a Klargester 2,600 litre cesspit, about 12ft high with a square lid. Police say the thieves must have used a vehicle to steal it.

Peterborough Evening Telegraph

IDEAL FIRST PURCHASE £122,000

Kingston Property Weekly

WE REPORT TODAY on the astonishing rise in the number of children in London who receive home tutoring to help them get into the sedondary school of their choice and to pass examinations.

Evening Standard

HAMPDEN ROAD, N8

A two bedroom, two reception conversion close to Hornsey British Rail and Turnpike Lane tube.

£120,000 L/H

Advertisement, Haringey Advertiser

CUSTOMS chiefs are celebrating a "significant blow" to drug dealers after seizing cocaine worth £38 million.

Coventry Evening Telegraph

Australian police hold two over bushfires

Daily Telegraph

Hamiltons to be shot into space

Midweek Visitor (Southport)

Attention teachers: Teacher? New to K wait? Then you need the Kuwait Union for New Teachers. Become a KUNT, your friend can be KUNTs too-

Kuwait Times

BLUNKETT LASHES OUT

by Our Home Affairs Staff
Pat Riot

MR DAVID BLUNKETT today warned ethnic minorities that they had to embrace "British cultural values" or risk internment under his new anti-terrorist legislation.

When asked to define mainstream British culture he told journalists, "I don't mean all that class-ridden Tory rubbish about British history and stuff like Shakespeare. No, what I am talking about are our quintessentially British institutions such as McDonald's, Starbucks, Rupert Murdoch, Buddy Holly, The Simpsons, Walt Disney, Frasier, Friends, Adidas and Enron Hubbard, the founder of the American Church of Bankrupty."

He continued, "The most important British institution of all is, of course, New Labour and it is vital that potential immigrants have a basic command of English. They must be able to use simple phrases such as 'I agree with everything Mr Blair says' and 'I will vote Labour in the next election'."

MILLIONS LOST IN NEW YORK TRAGEDY

by **Ike** and **Tina Brown**

OSAMA bin Laden has added another crime to his long list of atrocities, *writes Tina Brown*. Last night *Talk Magazine*, the symbol of all that was best about America, lay in ruins having collapsed without warning.

As Tina Brown surveyed the smouldering remains of her once-proud empire in the area now known as "sales zero", she declared, "There is no doubt that this is the work of al-Qaeda and the Taliban."

One minute the magazine was a flourishing business full of hundreds of adverts and dozens of exciting pieces. The next, it was a pile of rubbish. Or was it the other way round?

© *All sycophantic British newspapers.*

Letters to the Editor

The Death of George Harrison MBE

SIR – I was appalled to see you devoting 38 pages of your once-great newspaper to the death of George Harrison. How out-of-touch can you get? Surely your readers deserved at least 80 pages on the passing of one of the world's greatest musicians and spiritual leaders?

Sir Harry Krishna
Dunmeditatin, Berks

SIR – I am sure that many Telegraph readers will have been as shocked as I was by the news that the late George Harrison had been cremated in a Hindu-style ceremony and his ashes mingled with the Holy river of the Ganga. Surely Mr Blair should have stepped in to insist that there should have been a full State Funeral for one of the greatest Englishmen who ever lived. The people of Britain have thus been cruelly denied the opportunity to hear the choir of Westminster Abbey singing such immortal compositions as "Taxman", "Something" and "Something Else".

Lord Krishna of Hari
Chantings, Glos

SIR – To many of us who grew up in the Sixties, the figure of J.R. Hartley was the background to our lives. Who of us can ever forget the first time we heard him asking for his new book "Fly Fishing" in the second-hand bookshop? From then on he was a living icon to a whole generation. We dressed like him, we spoke like him and we could all recite by heart the words of his immortal TV commercial "We All Live In The Yellow Pages". Surely the empty plinth in Trafalgar Square has now got an obvious candidate to stand alongside Havelock, Napier and Nelson Mandela.

Chris Na
The Old Riverbank, St Ickleback, Dorset

SIR – Alas your 16-page obituary of the late George Harrison was disfigured by many historical and technical errors. The most glaring of these was your obituarist's claim that Harrison's harmonic modulations in the opening bars of "My Guitar Gently Weeps" were heavily influenced by the 12-bar bridge passage in the middle of the 1928 classic Potato Pickin' Momma Blues recorded by Alabama legend Blind Lemon Shandy Levine in 1936. As Harrison himself made clear in his famous interview with me for the Hamburg magazine *Blaues und Blauemenschen* (Blues and Bluesmen) in 1973, the original B♭ 7th to E♭ 7th progression was given to him by his Quarry Bank schoolfriend Sir George Harrison Birtwhistle (as he later became) in 1959. If anyone is interested in further musicological data on Harrison's early influences, I refer them to my website www.dullbore.com

Jan Arak
Den Haag, Nederlands

"Well, someone must have wanted this meeting"

YE TIMES OF LONDON

November 4, 1605

Editor: Mafter Peter Stoatherd Efq. Lickfpittle Extraordinary to Ye Dirtie Diggerfrom Ye Undifcovered Colony of Auftralia

GUY FAWKES TO BE GIVEN OFFICE IN YE HOUSES OF PARLIAMENT

YE WORLD of Weftminfter was rocked to its foundations yefterday, by ye newes that Mafter Guy Fawkes, a well-known Papift and fcoundrel, hath been given all ye facilities of ye Houfe of Commons, including an allowance of 12 groats a yeare and a cafe of sack.

MORTAL SINN FEIN

Mafter Fawkes hath chosen an office in ye cellars, and hath requefted to be granted 36 barrels, 18 bushels of finest gunpowder and a box of ye newe-fangled phofphorous matches (as brought back from ye Newe Worlde by Sir Walter Raleigh, to light up ye pipe-full of tobacco).

Only one voice was heard protefting against ye decision by ye government — to wit Mafter Duncan Smith, ye new leader of ye Tory faction.

BEWARE YE IDS OF NOVEMBER

Mafter Smith coughed pafsionately for several minutes, before declaring "thif marks the ende of ye bipartifan approach which we have followed since ye time of Henry VIII".

But quoth a defiant Guido Fawkes, "This is a fufs about nothing. It hath been all blown up out of proportion."

ON OTHER PAGES

Mafter Coren contributes his usual witty column about late events in ye remote village of Cricklewood. Page 14

Mafter Parrish "Why I Am Giving Up Ye Parliamentary Sketch – Because Nothing Happeneth There Anymore. Page 21

Unfunny Cartoon by Rubens

WEST BELFAST SCHOOL of IRISH DANCING

MCLACHLAN

"Decommission the arms, please, Siobhan"

THIS WEEK

NO. 94
TERENCE CONRAN

(This feature was held over from our last issue as it was considered inappropriate to publish it in the light of world circumstances at the time.)

Would you say that spoons had changed a lot in your lifetime?

I don't think young people today can have any conception how provincial and dreary British spoons were in the 50s. It was only in the 60s when we opened Habitat and I introduced Danish, Italian and Swedish spoons to this country that the whole culture of spoons took off.

Do you take credit for changing the face of spoons?

Of course. We did it with deckchairs, sofas, coffee-grinders. We showed that an object could be functional and beautiful at the same time. Our range of stripped-pine spoons sold over 30 million in the first year. For the first time Britain was serious about spoons.

I suppose, as a perfectionist, you take particular care to get the spoons right in all your many restaurants?

I'm currently replacing all the spoons in my restaurants with a very exciting new range by the brilliant young Irish-Japanese designer Brendan Suzuki.

And what are they like, these new spoons?

At first sight they look exactly like the kind of cheap and cheerful spoons you get given in airport buffets. But then, that's the whole point. They're cutting-edge retro. It's the sort of thing I'm famous for. It's up to the customers to keep up.

So, is there a definitive Conran spoon?

Everything I do is definitive. Food, lifestyle, spoons. It's what the world expects from Conran.

Has anything amusing ever happened to you in connection with a spoon?

Well, actually, yes. When I opened Ripoff in Covent Garden, David Hockney drew a spoon on the tablecloth and…

… you mean 'No'?

NEXT WEEK: Sir Simon Rattle – "Me and My Toaster".

THE RETURN OF THE SPARTS

Who Are They, The Sinister Left-Wingers Who Want To Bring Britain To Its Knees?

by Timesman **Michael Goverthetop**

WE THOUGHT we had seen the last of the tightly-knit group of die-hard Trotskyist militants whose aim was to overthrow Britain's democracy and set up a Stalinist dictatorship in its stead. But now they are back. Make no mistake, the madmen of the left have returned with a vengeance and, like rats, this time they are stronger and more virulent than ever before.

Total Rubbish

● Here they are – the evil men who could destroy our way of life for ever:

Mick Spart, 57, senior shop steward of the powerful TEACUP union, currently in dispute with Connex North Central over Toilet Tissue Allowances for Non-Driving Auxiliary Personnel.

Eric Spart, 38, part-time A-Level Media Studies supply teacher at Neasden's notorious Robert Mugabe Comprehensive School.

Louise Spartian, 38, radical left-wing lawyer who regularly represents guilty clients on political grounds. Has appeared on "Question Time", criticising Stephen Byers and getting a round of applause.

Paul Spart, 61, notorious anarchist agitator and journalist who writes a weekly column for the influential "Sparts and Spartsmen" magazine (circulation 3).

Jeremy Sparty, 49, Stalinist stand-up comedian and regular guest on the subversive radio programme "Gardeners' Question Time". Once wrote letter to Guardian making joke about President Bush.

(That's enough Sparts. Ed.)

Cherie Blair *Not* At Public Event Shock

by Our Political Staff **U. Biquitous**

CHERIE Blair surprised onlookers at an event yesterday when she failed to make an appearance or be photographed for the newspapers.

The Prime Minister's wife stunned the organisers of the event by not arriving wearing an ethnic costume or a new trouser suit and then not chatting happily to celebrities like Kate Winslet or Harry Potter.

"It was incredible," said one spokesman, "Cherie wasn't there looking marvellous and being wonderfully natural with the children or the old people or whoever they were."

Celebrity Blairs

A Downing Street spokesman, however, issued a statement at once, saying, "Although Cherie Blair tries to be everywhere at all times, it is possible that she did miss this event due to being at another one."

Queen Cherie is 49.

BLAIR TO SET UP INQUIRY INTO 'BLOODY SUNDAY INQUIRY'

by Our Political Staff **Londonderry Irvine** and **Bloody Mary Kenny**

THE Government is to hold a top-level public inquiry into what ministers were last night describing as "one of the most shocking atrocities in the history of Northern Ireland".

Its aim will be to establish precisely what happened on that fateful day all those years ago when hundreds of highly-trained professional lawyers arrived in the city of Londonderry and began recklessly charging huge fees in all directions.

Hundreds of millions of pounds simply vanished, as the lawyers became responsible for the greatest waste of money in the long and bloody history of the legal profession.

Derry And Tommies

The chief concern of the inquiry will be to investigate the controversial role played by prime minister Tony Blair, who ordered in the lawyers "without thinking through the inevitable consequences of such a shamelessly political act".

The new inquiry, which is likely to last for several hundred years, will be held in the Millennium Dome and chaired by a leading independent lawyer, Ms Cherie Booth QC, who will receive a nominal fee of £1 million a day.

The Grauniad

We Name The Guilty Men Of Omagh

There is no secret about who is to blame for this terrible atrocity. It is the police. The Guardian says: They should all be strung up, it's the only language they understand.

© *Rubbishertrash 2001.*

GREAT PHILOSOPHERS OF HISTORY

No. 94 Scrutonides

SCRUTONIDES, whose school briefly flourished in the late 20th century, held that the highest good could only be attained by those who were dedicated to the pure pursuit of knowledge for its own sake, unsullied by any material consideration such as receiving money from commercial organisations. His celebrated axiom "Fumo ergo sum" ("I smoke therefore I am very rich") was much-quoted until Scrutonides was revealed as a charlatan who had himself received payment from tobacco companies. He retired

and spent his declining years in a barrel.

U.S. PRISONERS

Confused, disoriented, and with no idea what is happening

That's no way to talk about the President

WAR ON PRETZELS
━━ DAY 94 ━━

■ **U.S. Special Forces round up suspected pretzel salesmen and deport them to a military base on Cuba.**

■ **Man arrested on aeroplane carrying pretzel concealed in his shoe.**

■ **Blair makes speech pledging S.A.S. troops to help fight the international pretzel menace.**

■ **Documents found in Kabul reveal Do-It-Yourself Pretzel Assembly Manual in possession of al-Qaeda.**

■ **Britons may have been trained in the use of pretzels.**

■ **American warplanes destroy "Cheesy Wotsit" factory in Slough by mistake, killing hundreds of innocent** *(That's enough War On Pretzels. Ed.)*

A Taxi Driver writes

THIS WEEK: **Dave Yelland** (Cab No. 3246) on the rights of the al-Qaeda prisoners-of-war held at Guantanamo Bay, Cuba.

Well, stands to reason, how can they be prisoners-of-war when there wasn't even a bloody war – not a real war like England v. Germany in the World Cup, I mean, they go on about human rights, but we didn't hear much about that when the Taliban blew up those giant Buddhists, did we? I mean anyone can say they're an army, just because they've got a towel on their head and wave a gun around, I mean even the Kray brothers could have called themselves a bleedin' army, guv, I had that Ronnie in the back of the cab once, a lovely gentleman, he put a gun to my head and nicked all my takings.

NEXT WEEK: Borry Johnson on You Can Stuff The Euro Up Your Eu-Know Where!!!

At least I'm not in a British hospital

Axis of Evil

"Does my bomb look big in this?"

POLLY FILLER

ON NIGELLA

SO women are supposed to be suffering from Nigella-Induced Dinner Party Stress Anxiety (NIDPSA), brought on by our fear of failing to live up to the standards of the Domestic Goddess? Oh pur-leeeese!

As someone who has just done lunch for 11 adults and 13 children (plus three dogs and a cat!!) I can tell you, Nigella, it's not as hard as you make it look!! At the end of the four-course meal (mmm, delicious!!!) a group of close friends and colleagues (including the editor of this paper) charged their glasses and drank to a toast to "Polly, the Domestic Goddess"!

I'm embarrassed to mention it but like any good reporter I have to tell it how it was! And more than one guest asked me, "Polly, why on earth haven't they given you a TV series yet?" But according to all these reports in the papers, I was meant to be in the loony bin having a nervous breakdown! What rubbish!

So, how did I manage to out-Nigella Nigella! Well, it wasn't with any help from a certain useless "new man", who spent the entire morning watching the World Penguin Wrestling Championship from Antarctica presented by Paul Ross. (Thanks Simon!)

NO, the whole feast was put on by yours truly, *toute seule* and on my ownsome! And like sensible women all over the country I wasn't reduced to tears by the thought of living in Nigella's shadow – even though it's quite a big one and it's getting bigger by the day!?! Especially round the hips!?! Actually I've got a recipe for you, Nigella! How about salad and tap water for a change? That should do the trick!

So let's hear no more about NIDPSA!? And let's not put Nigella on a pedestal – it'll probably collapse under the strain! Instead let's salute ourselves: the ordinary working women of Britain ! (And Notting Hill's elite catering service at www.yourfeetup.com)

Happy New Year!

Pollyella

Coming soon on Channel 4

100 Best Spoons

YOU THE viewers vote on the world's top spoons from a list prepared by the British Spoon Institute (BSI). Will the overall spoon winner be the classic Citizen Spoon from Habitat or will it be the futuristic Star Spoon from Ikea? Graham Norton presides over this innuendo-packed festival of spoonery. "I've got a long one," he says, "and I'm going to dip it in a cup of tea."

The Daily Talibangraph

Friday, December 28, 2001

MYSTERY DEEPENS OVER WHEREABOUTS OF BIN DUNCAN

By Our Special Correspondent Al Campbell

London, Tuesday

IN THE depths of the Tory Bory complex there are the scattered remains of a handful of fanatical supporters – but the man himself is nowhere to be found.

There have been occasional sightings of the fanatical leader of a once powerful ruling sect but nothing concrete has been heard of him for months.

A video purporting to be of Bin Duncan addressing the House of Commons has been released but the sound is very bad and the content of Bin Duncan's speech is very hazy and out of focus.

Conspiracy theorists believe that the video is a fake and that the man purporting to be Bin Duncan is a body double – probably called Francis Wheen.

In his last recorded radio transcript on the respected Al-Steve-Wright-In-The-Afternoon-Show, Bin Duncan can be heard exhorting his troops, "to give in at all costs and admit that Tony Blair will defeat them."

Some people claim Bin Duncan is already dead in the water, others that he is in hiding deep in Smith Square. One thing is sure. No one knows or cares.

TEENAGER SMOKED POT AND HAD TOO MUCH TO DRINK

by Our Entire Staff

A 16-year-old boy went several times to a pub and smoked a joint in a shed outside.

(Reuters)

INSIDE

- That teenage boy story in full **2-6**
- Hundreds of pics of teenage boy **7-8**
- Blurred pics of boy's friends **9**
- Is it every parent's worst nightmare? *ask 15 of our top columnists* **10-16**
- What's all the fuss about, for Heaven's sake? *ask the other* 15 **17-26**
- Does teenage drinking and pot-smoking lead to terminal insanity? *asks Dr Thomas Utterfraud* **27**
- Should the police have arrested the teenage boy? *ask 100 of our top reporters* **28-32**
- Bring back flogging for teenage boy, say 78% of London's cabbies **33**
- Leading article – "Why Teenage Boy Is A Lesson For Us All" **34**
- "Have We All Gone Stark Staring Mad?" *asks Paul Johnson, "I Know I Have."* **35**

"What is it, dear... You and Michael don't seem as close"

A GLENDA SLAGG SPECIAL

Fleet Street's Columnist Of The Year (1973) Speaks Out On The Burning Issue Of The Day

■ HATS OFF to Prince Charles for a first-class piece of modern parenting!!?!! No dad could have handled the situation better!?!! Faced with a teenage son who'd gone a bit wild in the school hols, he could have done his nut and thrashed the boy within an inch of his life. Many would have said he deserved it. But not me, mister!?!!

And I speak as one who has been there, done it and got the T-shirt?!?

You showed your concern and your compassion by sending the boy to a drug-rehabilitation clinic, to see for himself the horrors which drugs can wreak on the impressionable youngster of today.

Well done, sire!!!!?!

■ PRINCE CHARLES!?! There's only one word for him. A complete fool!?!?

Is it any wonder that his son has been turned into a crazed drug addict, when he has for years been ignored by his callous, vain, womanising, selfish fool of a father? If only Charles had stayed at home and listened to his son's problems, as any caring father would have done, Prince Harry would still be alive today.

■ *PRINCE HARRY! Aren'tchasickofhim?!!? Just because he's a spoiled rich kid, he can behave like a yob and get away with it!!!?!!*

If it was your kid or mine, he'd have been banged up in a cell, looking at the wrong end of a 10-year sentence?!??

Go on, Prince Hooray!! Scram!!!

■ THREE CHEERS for Prince Harry! This handsome hunk has shown that the Royals are just like the rest of us!!?!!?

Not for him the cloistered world of cucumber sandwiches and croquet for tea with the toffee-nosed brigade!?!

No, this People's Prince for the 21st Century is down the boozer, knocking back the pints and smoking the odd spliff with his mates. Well done, your Royal Highness!!!?!

Byeeee!!

"I think it's time you and I had a little chat"

WHEN HARRY MET DADDY

He's learnt his lesson

Er... what's that?

I won't get caught next time

School news
St Hashcakes

Marijuana Term begins today. There are 1,207 users in the school. R.S.J. Dope-Ffiend (Rizlas) is Keeper of the Stash. P.L.R. Pothead (Roaches) is Captain of Reefers. Mr L.S. Dealer replaces Dr Methadone as Head of Chemistry. He will be organising the school trip. The Bong will be held on The Grass on 23rd February. There will be a performance of the School Play ("Trainspotting") in the Uppers Hall on 7th March. Tickets can be obtained from the Bursar, Wing Commander "Spliffy" Spliffington O.C. Ecstasies will be on 7th March.

THE DAILY TUDORGRAPH

10 Groats (or 26.42 euros) ———— Friday January 25

CONCERN GROWS OVER YE LOW COMPANIONS OF YE PRINCE HARRY

by Ye Editor Of Ye Tudorgraph
ST CHARLES MOORE

MAKE no miftake about it, ye throne of England hath been rocked to its foundations by ye lateft shock revelations concerning ye drinking habits of Prince Hal, ye royal perfonage.

According to ye Newes Of Ye Known World, ye Prince hath been reforting to a lowe tavern in Eastcheap, Ye Boare's Head, where he hath been caroufing long into ye night with a crewe of lewd and licentious reprobates.

Who are they? We name ye guilty parties who hath led ye innocent prince into a life of shameless debauchery and crime:

• Mafter JACK FALSTAFF, a notorious haunter of ale houfes and ftudent at ye Royal College of Agriculture in ye ancient market town of Cirencester.

• Mafter BARDOLPH, a notorious rake and reprobate, alfo ftudying land management at ye Royal College

• Miftress DOLL TARA PALMER-TOMKINSON, a wench and hussey who is faid to be "no better than she should be".

But whilft Prince Harry difporteth himself with his crew of vagabonds, the queftion on every lip is – when will Harry's father take ye boy firmly in hand and fend him for professional counfelling? (Surely "have his head cut off?" Ed.)

Tomorrow: Henry IV Part Two. Referve your copy now!

Ye Prince & Companion On Way To Ye Pubbe

ON OTHER PAGES

✳ Ye 100 Yeares War Breaks Out page 2

✳ Ye Blacke Deathe – Yes, It's Back! page 3

✳ Who Shoulde Be Ye New Archbishop Of Canterbury – Ye Choose! page 8

✳ Introducing Our Neweste Columnist, Mafter William Deedes page 10

"It takes ages to get in since they scrapped admission charges"

MMR LATEST

Have you had the injection?

It's none of your business

What You Didn't Hear

The Today Programme

Sue McGhastly *(for it is she)*: ... thank you, John. It's 7.43, and we move on to the controversial topic of 'Kiss And Tell' memoirs. Should the private secrets of the pillow be peddled for profit? In the studio we have broadcaster Sue MacGregor, who has just published her life story, *My Naughtie, Naughtie Nights...*

Sue MacGregor *(for it is also she)*: ... that's right, Sue. It's available in all good bookshops...

McGhastly: It's all very well to make a joke of it, Miss MacGregor, but a lot of people have been very upset by your account of sleeping with the married actor Leonard Rossiter. How on earth can you justify putting all that in?

MacGregor: Well, I was under a lot of pressure from my publisher. He said 300 pages describing how I drank coffee out of plastic cups with John Humphrys and Brian Redhead wasn't going to sell any copies...

McGhastly: ...yes, well, that's as may be, but...

MacGregor: ...no, let me finish. He asked me if I could think of anything to spice it up a bit, so that they could sell the serialisation to the *Daily Mail*.

McGhastly: So you're admitting that you just betrayed these confidences for money? And the widow, Mrs Rossiter, apparently knew nothing about it. Is that right?

MacGregor: Well, that's a very crude way of putting it, but...

McGhastly: ... so it's true? Some people might say that you were just an unscrupulous, greedy, shameless old scrubber. How do you respond to that? And I must ask you to be brief, since we've only got two seconds left, which are now up.

MacGregor: ... er...

McGhastly: Sorry, that's all we've got time for. And now it's time for Thought For The Day, with Mr Rodney Spruce, who is Reader in Satanic Studies at the University of Melton Mowbray (formerly the Institute of Mechanically Recovered Meat).

Mr Spruce: When I heard the news from India of England's victory in the latest one-day cricket match, I couldn't help feeling, as I am sure all my fellow Satanists did, that life is rather like that, and...

(Continued on 94 KHz)

That Edexcel Exam Paper In Full

GCSE BIOLOGY

Candidates must answer 7 of the following 4 questions. Write on all three sides of the paper. You have 2½ seconds.

1. Explain the difference between the following parts of the human body:

a) The arse

b) The elbow

4. If you were unable to answer question one, would you like a job at Edexcel?

STARS FLOCK TO ANDY ARSHOL PARTY

by **Alastair Campbell's Soup**

YES! They were all there. The icons of the Sixties that you hoped you would never see again.

And they were all gathered at the Tat Modern Gallery in London to celebrate the world's greatest artist Andy Arshol.

Guests who partied late into the night, dancing to the cult Sixties band "The Who Cares", included:

● **Marianne Unfaithfull**
● **Nicky Hasbeen**
● **Brian Ono**
● **Salman Washdup**

And a host of other people you can't remember.

Said the Tat Modern supremo Sir Nicholas Arsota, "This party symbolises exactly what Andy Arshol meant as an artist. You don't want to be here for more than 15 minutes."

What You Will See

● **Picture of Baked Bean tin**
● **Picture of Marilyn Monroe coloured yellow**
● **Er... that's it.**

PRINCESS MARGARET

A NATION DOESN'T MOURN

by Our Entire Staff Phil Supplement

AS A mark of respect, the entire nation carried on as normal yesterday, after the death was announced of Her Royal Highness Princess Margaret.

"It is just like Diana all over again," said no one, as two small bouquets of flowers were laid at the palace railings by newspaper photographers desperate for some kind of a picture to mark the occasion.

Flags flew at half-mast, cathedral bells sounded muffled peals and millions of ordinary people failed to observe a minute's silence as they queued to get into their local supermarket.

The Poet Laureate Marks The Passing Of Her Royal Highness With A Moving Verse Tribute

Death Of A Princess
by SIR ANDREW GOINGTHROUGHTHEMOTION

So. Farewell then
Princess Margaret.
Torn between love and
Duty.
A life unfulfilled.
The rebellious conformist.
Trapped bird in
A royal cage.
Poor little
Rich girl.
Will this
Do?   (A.M.)

PRINCESS Margaret had the misfortune to be born a princess. It was a truly tragic fate which denied her the chance to excel in almost any walk of life she might have chosen.

Those of us who had the privilege of knowing her were constantly in awe at the extraordinary range of her talents and learning.

She could easily, for instance, have been an Oxford don, and had read almost every book printed in the English language.

The Bible she knew by heart, and had it not been for her sex, she would have been a strong candidate to become the first female Archbishop of Canterbury.

Her wit was legendary, and she was often compared to Oscar Wilde, Dorothy Parker and TV's Alan Coren.

"Who's that common little man with a cigar?" she once asked, pointing at Sir Winston Churchill.

Anyone who heard her play *Chopsticks* would have known at once that she had formidable gifts as a pianist which, had fate decreed otherwise, could have put her up alongside Arthur Rubinstein or Vladimir Horovitz.

And that is to ignore her wonderful singing. She knew all the songs from the shows, and could be prevailed upon at a soiree to sing "Wouldn't it be luvverly" in an amusing cockney voice.

She was furthermore probably the greatest 20th Century expert on classical ballet, and her gift for smoking was (cont'd. p. 94)

Was She The World's Most Talented Woman?

asks Paul Johnson

Princess Margaret Cremated

*"It's a **really** nice area"*

Those Joan Collins Vows In Full

Vicar: Do you take this cheque for £400,000?

Collins: OK.

Vicar: You may now kiss your husband goodbye.

IN THE COURTS

The Case of Her Royal Highness the Naomi of Campbell v. The Daily Moron

Day 94

Before Mr Justice Cocklecarrot

The case continued today in which the world's most beautiful supermodel claimed that her privacy had been breached by a front-page report in the Daily Moron headlined 'Come Off It, Naomi – You're Just A Druggie Slag'.

For the Daily Moron, Mr Desmond Brownnose QC asked the editor of the Daily Moron, Mr Piers Moron, how he could justify the publication of the article.

Mr Brownnose QC: Mr Moron, you are a distinguished and highly-respected journalist, are you not?

Moron: No, I am not.

Brownnose: We agreed you would say "yes" at this point.

Moron: Oh yes, sorry Des.

Mr Justice Cocklecarrot: Miss Campbell, if you would find it easier to follow the proceedings if you were sitting up here next to me, do feel free so to do. Pray continue, Sir Desmond.

Brownnose: I am indebted to Your Lordship.

Cocklecarrot: But not as indebted as you are to the Daily Moron for inviting you to represent them in this absurd case.

(Lawyers all dissolve in laughter at this example of judicial wit)

Brownnose: Very amusing, Your Lordship! Mr Moron, I put it to you that, in publishing this article, you were acting only out of the very highest motives, and out of a desire to serve the public interest in exposing a matter of supreme national importance?

Moron: If you say so, Des!

(The Court then heard the evidence of Miss Chocolate-Soldier)

Mr Andrew Hugefee QC *(for Ms Campbell)*: Miss Campbell, I know that this must be very difficult for you to put into words, but would you describe your feelings at seeing your photograph in the newspaper as being ones of intense agony, humiliation, shame and suicidal depression?

Ms Campbell: Yes, I am a drug addict.

Hugefee: That is the answer to the next question.

Campbell: Oh, shit.

Cocklecarrot: I can well understand, my dear, your feelings of frustration and confusion with all these beastly lawyers asking their horrid questions. Perhaps if you'd like to join me at the Garrick for luncheon, the court could adjourn. They do an awfully good Spotted Dick!

(The court then adjourned until half-past-three, when the cross-examination resumed of Ms Naomi Cokehead)

Mr Brownnose: Miss Cokesniffer, you are well-known, are you not, for your short temper and foul language?

Ms Campbell: Shut up, bumface.

Cocklecarrot: Mr Bumface, I can see you have unnecessarily distressed this delightful young lady. Miss Campbell, it seems to be getting rather hot in this courtroom. Should you feel more comfortable by removing your clothing, please do not let anyone stop you.

(The case continues)

'A VAIN, FOUL-MOUTHED MANIPULATOR OF THE TRUTH'

COURT'S HISTORIC VERDICT

A HIGH COURT judge yesterday branded one of Britain's top celebrities as "an unreliable witness who uses the press for personal publicity and who is given to coarse and vulgar temper tantrums".

Piers Morgan, he said, had told the court that he had printed pictures of Naomi Campbell "out of a duty to the public" which was demonstrably... *(Cont. p. 94)*

ON OTHER PAGES

● **Piers Morgan** on his shameful addiction to shares – "Yes, I am an addict," he admits, "but I am trying to clean up my act."

GLENDA SLAGG

FLEET STREET'S BITTER CHOCOLATE SOLDIER!!!

■ NAOMI CAMPBELL!!!!? Ha! Ha! Ha! At last this brainless bimbo has been put in her place by winning her court case against the Daily Mirror *(Surely some mistake? Ed.)*. This guttersnipe in a glitzy gown has learned her lesson at last!!?!? Don't mess with the press, OK??!?

■ THREE cheers for the judge who put the drug-crazed catwalk queen in her place!!?! That'll teach her to go to court and win!???! Privacy??!? Don't make me laugh, darling!!?!? Now we'll come round and take a photo of you on the toilet if we feel like it??!?! Geddit??!??! *(This is great. More please. Ed.)*

BUSH DECLARES WAR ON ENRONIA

by Our Diplomatic Staff **N. Ron Hubbard**

White House, Tuesday

IN HIS State of the Onion address last night, the President of the United States declared war on "an evil regime that is threatening to destabilise the American government".

Mr Bush described the Enron leadership as "a fanatical group of folks hell bent on bringing down the entire American caboodle".

He accused them of "terrorising him" and "launching a suicidal assault on my administration".

THE ENRON IS NIGH

Critics of the President have pointed out that it was the U.S. Government which originally backed the Enron movement and its fundamentally greedy leaders. They argue that the close links with the U.S. Government were to blame for the creation of the Enron/Ar-Thuranderson network in the first place.

But the President was unmoved. He declared all-out war on Enronia and ordered B-52 bombers in to destroy all documents linking him to the scandal.

The British Prime Minister, Tony Blair, last night said that he "stood shoulder to shoulder with the President up to his neck in it."

THAT SPEECH IN FULL

Happy Christmas to y'all!

Today we face an axis of evil stretching across the galaxy, an evil empire led by Darth Bin Vader and his Comanches, intent on destroying our American way of life, our hot dog stands, our apple pie and our Kentucky Fried McMuffins. So who are they, these evil countries?

I have a list of them in front of me right here. Iran, Iraq, Iroquois, North Korea, North Dakota, North by North West, Northern Ireland, the lost city of Atlantis and El Dorado...

(At this point, Mr Bush was injected with anti-pretzel serum, rendering him temporarily conscious.)

God bless Enronia!

"Oh no!"

ENRON SCANDAL

Power corrupts and power companies corrupt absolutely...

The Enron Accounting System

CHAFF.

Verses To Mark The Heroic Outlawing Of Hunting With Hounds North Of The Border

 BY WILLIAM REES-MCGONAGALL

'Twas in the year two-thousand-and-two
That the Scottish Parliament at last showed what
it could do!
When the heirs of those great reformers Calvin
and Knox
Finally managed to ban the hunting of the fox.

For centuries past, Scotland had borne no greater shame
Than the ruthless pursuit of bushy-tailed game,
As the sassenach lairds with their baying hounds
Had chased the fox o'er all Scotland's holy grounds.

Never was known such a cruel and barbarous sport
As when puir wee Reynard by the English dogs
was caught.
Never in history had so much innocent blood stained
the heather
Nor were the huntsmen constrained by the vagaries
of the weather.

But then at last the bravehearts of the Scottish
Assembly
Showed all the courage of Scotland's football fans
when they travel down to Wembley
And with a mighty cry of "Ye'll no gang hunting
nae more"
On this terrible infringement of animal rights they
slammed the door.

Meanwhile 400 miles away in London town
No wonder prime minister Blair was wearing a
fearful frown.
For the gallant MSPs had shown him the way
And he said "I'll do the same myself – some other day."

GAYS BACK TORIES

by Our Political Staff **Matthew Gay Paris**

IN A dramatic u-turn, homosexuals yesterday said that in future they would respect the rights of other people "to be practising Tories".

"Many decent people," said a spokesman, "from all walks of life have owned up to having Conservative leanings and it is time we accepted this minority view as normal.

"For too long," he continued, "we have been guilty of looking at Tories as if they were deviant freaks who deserved our pity and could be cured if only they met the right member of the Labour party.

"Let's live and let live," he concluded, "and as a mark of how far we have come, I am going to shake hands with Oliver Letwin."

Michael Portillo must be livid.

'FAT CATS' TO CLOSE

by Our Showbiz Staff
William Rees-Moggy

AFTER twenty-one years of delighting its accountants, the long-running West End show 'Fat Cats' is to come to an end.

The legendary spectacular, featuring Cameron Mackintosh and Andrew Lloyd Webber, set new standards in the world of money with its charming story of two lovable Fat Cats who get incredibly rich. Who can forget numbers like £136 million in London? $500 million on Broadway? Or 1000 billion euros worldwide?

Said a tearful Andrew Lloyds Bank last night, "All good things have to come to an end. And some things that aren't any good do as well."

SPEAKER LASHES COMMONS 'SNOBS'

by Our Political Staff **Andrew Marrtin**

THE SPEAKER of the House of Commons, Mr Michael Martin, today hit out at his critics whom, he said, "Look down their noses at the likes of me."

Mr Martin complained that he was the victim of discrimination and was being pilloried simply because he was "useless".

Working Arse

He told reporters, "Just because I am not up to the job, that is no reason to criticise me. People who are useless have as much right to be Speaker as those who aren't.

"It's all down to the way I speak," he continued. "The snobs have got it in for me because when I open my mouth I talk nonsense. I can't help that. It's the way I am.

"It's all down to class," he concluded. "I haven't got any – unlike Betty Boothroyd, George Thomas and all those other snooty toffs who had the job before *(continued p. 94)*

"Ordure! Ordure!"

Campaign to save albatross launched

If we don't act soon, he and his kind will be completely extinct

LORD HOLLICK TO RUN SOUTH BANK

by Our Arts Correspondent **Elizabeth Hall**

THE Prime Minister's friend Lord Hollick is to take charge of the crisis-ridden Arts Complex on the South Bank.

Following his success in running the Daily Express, Lord Hollick has announced the following exciting 5-point plan to transform London's premier cultural venue.

1. Sell it all off to Richard "Dirty" Desmond.

2. Festival Hall to become Lap-Dancing Centre.

3. Hayward Gallery to exhibit hardcore pornography, featuring Asian Babes, etc.

4. National Theatre to be turned into a warehouse for unsold copies of *OK!* magazine.

5. Er... That's it.

COURT CIRCULAR

GOSFORD PARK

Their Royal Highnesses the Earl and Countess of Wessex will be receiving a cheque from Her Majesty the Queen for £1 million. This will be followed by their immediate retirement from professional life. The Earl has graciously agreed not to film his nephew on the toilet and the Countess has consented not to discuss Royal matters with *News of the World* journalists dressed up as Sheikhs.

SOUTHFORK LODGE

The Duchess Fergiana is to relaunch herself in the pages of the *Hello!* magazine. Readers will discover that she is thinner than she was and is to embark on a new career of appearing in *Hello!* magazine and telling everyone how thin she is.

HIGHGROVE

His Royal High the Prince Harry will receive Inspector Knacker of the Drugs Squad, who will graciously grant him a Royal Pardon. He will then celebrate with a number of pints of snakebite with the Inebriate-in-Waiting the Honourable Guy Perry Worsthorne.

ST ANDREWS

His Royal Highness the Prince of Hearts will attend a lecture at which he will get rather bored. He will then proceed to sit in his room feeling sorry for himself and watching afternoon television. He will then ring His Royal Highness the Prince of Wales, who will tell him "If you think *you're* bored, you should try being the Prince of Wales." A brief altercation will ensue, during which HRH the Prince William will say "It's *so* unfair" (© H. Enfield)

WOGGAWOGGALAND

His Royal Highness the Duke of Edinburgh will meet a number of aboriginal gentlemen with spears. He will then follow time-honoured Royal tradition and will make an offensive remark about their modern-day role *(That's enough. Ed.)*

MUGABE SWEEPS TO VICTORY

by Our Man Not In Harare Because He's Been Killed

PRESIDENT Mugabe last night took the unusual step of issuing next month's election results in advance.

"This action is necessary," he told himself, "to stop the media misinterpreting the results to suggest that I did not win. The world will see that all is fair and above board and there was no need for any outside observers of the type who might have unfortunately been murdered if they had stayed."

Those Results In Full

His Supreme Holiness King Comrade Robert Mugabe I (Democratic Freedom Party) *25 million (everyone)*

The late Mr Morgan Tsvangirai (Anti-Democratic Tool of Western Capitalists and CIA Party) *0 (nobody – which is just as well since he is unfortunately dead due to a bad cold)*

BIG RON PICKS 'THE NEASDEN CLASSICS' CD

by **E.I. Erewego** Our Man In The Virgin Record Store With The Ear-Plugs And The Avocado-'n'-Custard Sarnie

TIGHT-LIPPED Neasden soccer supremo Ron Knee, 59, has put together his favourite pieces of classical music for a special CD to promote the North Circular World Cup Trophy.

Big Ron, 59, told reporters, "It has given me hours of pleasure to select my all-time classical favourites and I hope millions of people will enjoy listening to them for the first time, as I have done."

Symphony Number Sven

That Ron Knee Collection in full:
● You'll Never Walk Alone (Elgar)
● Nice One, Cyril (Delius)

● Aria: 'E I Addio' from Mozart's Don Revianni

Already the fans (Sid and Doris Bonkers) have given the CD their thumbs up. "We shall definitely be thinking of buying the set. It's great value at £29.99," said Sid.

LATE SCORE

Brahms Academicals 7

Schubert Wanderers 3

SOLDIERS KILLED IN WAR SHOCK

SEVEN American soldiers have died fighting in a war (*Reuters*).

On other pages

● U.S. in shock at deaths **6**

● "This must never happen again" – Bush's pledge **8**

● Is it another Vietnam? asks

● everybody **10-14**

● What happens when soldiers die – Dr Thomas Stuttaford **16**

THE WIFE OF RILEY

NOT ONLY . . . . BUT ALSO . . .

PETER COOK R.I.P.

DUDLEY MOORE R.I.P

RSJ

DUDLEY MOORE

Exclusive To All Newspapers

IT's goodbyee to the pint-sized cuddly comic who became a sex thimble... Dagenham... club foot... Hollywood... four wives... sex-symbol... pint-sized... cuddly... Arthur... Hollywood... Bo Derek... Dagenham... Hollywood...
(continued on page 94)

Not On Other Pages

Oxford organ scholar and celebrated jazz pianist dies...

SUNDAY TIMES INSIGHT SPECIAL

The chain of events that led to the biggest scandal the world has ever seen.

Thursday 8.25am Martin Sixpence, the Head of Paperclips at the Department of Transport sends an e-mail to his colleague Jo Mooron, Special Adviser to the Special Adviser to Stephen Byebye, Secretary of State for Transport. The explosive e-mail advises Mooron not to issue any press releases on Friday even if she wasn't thinking of doing so.

Thursday 12.00pm The e-mail is leaked to the highly influential political correspondent of the Daily Moron, Paul Glasses. When the story appears, it causes a sensation.

Friday 7.10am A plainly shaken Jo Mooron denies the e-mail ever existed. She is supported by Stephen Byebye, who says he will stand by her.

Friday 2.30pm A distinctly rattled Robin Cook tells the House that there was never any e-mail from Sixpence and even if there was, no one had ever seen it. He promises that the Government will stand by Mooron and Sixpence.

Friday 4.00pm As the scandal continues unabated, the Prime Minister steps in to deny that anyone ever denied that an e-mail had been sent. He promises to stand by Cook, Mooron and Sixpence, unless something else happens.

Saturday 6.30am Something else happens. The text of the e-mail is printed in full in the Indescribablyboring newspaper. It reads, "Jo, have you got enough paperclips in your department?"

Saturday 5.00pm Everyone resigns (except for Blair).

HINDUJA, BYERS AND VAZ

I'm as innocent as you are, Keith

THE MEMO THAT PROVES MANDELSON IS INNOCENT

by Our Political Staff **Andrew Marrvelous**

A PREVIOUSLY unseen memo from a junior civil servant, Simon Jobsworth, has finally put Peter Mandelson in the clear over the so-called Hinduja-Passports-For-Dome-Cash Scandal.

The memo is now in the hands of Sir Wally Hammond QC, who produced the original report which exonerated everybody involved.

But now the Jobsworth memo opens the way for the return of Peter Mandelson to public life to resume his career as a man who gets sacked within a few weeks.

Says Sir Wally, "This is the clearest possible demonstration of Mr Mandelson's integrity and indeed my own in entirely ignoring its implications."

That Memo In Full

```
Dear Minister,
    If you want to put
in a word on behalf of
the H. Brothers with
M. O'B that would be
perfectly in order, so
long as a) you don't
do it in writing and
b) the press don't
find out. S.J.

(PS. I would destroy
this memo if I were
you or people will
think that you are up
to no good which you
are not of course, but
you know how people
talk.)
```

"Andrew's at a bit of a loose end. He'd planned to spend his gap year fighting for the Taliban"

GOVERNMENT ANNOUNCES EDUCATION SHAKE-UP

THE Education Minister Estelle Morris has unveiled a new scheme that will mean that schoolchildren will be able to by-pass their GCSEs.

"The system is known as truancy", said the clearly delighted minister, "and has been proved to ease over-crowding in the classroom whilst at the same time increasing the overall pass rate.

"We firmly believe that letting simple-minded infant thugs terrorise shopping centres during the day is the way forward for the British education system."

YES! IT'S VAZ

BRITAIN'S TOP COMIC

SLEAZY COME SLEAZY GO!

YOU'VE BEHAVED DISGRACEFULLY VAZ... YOU'LL PAY FOR THIS

NO I WON'T... THE HINDUJAS WILL... ...OR MR. MITTAL MAYBE...

SENIOR POLITICIAN

THAT'S IT! YOU'RE SUSPENDED FOR A MONTH!

THAT'S OUTRAGEOUS!

I SHOULD BE IN JAIL!!

BOOT!

ONLY KIDDING READERS!

RGJ

41

Lookalikes

Bin Laden   **Grace**

Sir,

Has anyone noticed the similarity between W.G. Grace and Osama bin Laden? Are they by any chance related?

Yours sincerely,
ANDREW MOBERLY
Henley on Thames, Oxon.

Spock   **Prince Charles**

Sir,

I wonder why Time magazine declined to publish David Hockney's portraits of Prince Charles, as recently released for auction. Surely, Time readers could have discerned that the accompanying article's references to aloof aliens, who only occasionally interbreed with the human race, were nothing to do with Mr Spock from Star Trek?

Yours faithfully,
STEVE ELLIS,
London E17.

e   **Sheikh Ahmed**

I wonder if by chance anyone has noticed the ...ilarity between Sheikh Ahmed Yassin, the guru ...he Palestinian Islamist movement Hamas, and ...ristopher Lee in the publicity stills for the Lord ...he Rings?

Having already played Jinnah and Fu ...nchu, can it only be a matter of time before the ...t Hammer ham plays the Palestinian ...lamentalists' spiritual leader?

JAMES GAVIN,
...e-mail.

Calf   **Lawson**

Sir,

Having purchased The Times' Saturday magazine to read about its cover star, the dogmatic goddess Pauline Calf, I was most disappointed to discover that it was merely a ruse exploiting the similarity between this celebrated TV beauty and the publication's own columnist Nigella Lawson.

Yours,
J.M. HOOD,
London E3.

Before   **After**

Sir,

Am I right in thinking the recent siege of Ramallah has taken an intolerable toll on Palestinian leader Yasser Arafat? Looks like he could use a holiday.

Yours etc,
Jen Eane.
Via email.

Warhol   **Ecclestone**

Sir,

Have you noticed the similarity between Andy Warhol and Bernie Ecclestone?

DAVID SCOTT,
Via e-mail.

Fayed   **Blofeld**

Sir,

Has anyone noticed the similarity between Mohammed Al Fayed and Ernst Stavro Blofeld - James Bond's nemesis. I wonder are they related?

MATTHEW CARSE,
Via email.

Interpreter   **Cut-Throat Jake**

Sir,

Have any of your readers noticed the similarity between the Taliban Mullah Zaeef's interpreter, and Cut-Throat Jake, the baddie in Captain Pugwash?

Yours faithfully,
CLAIR DENTON,
Bookham, Surrey.

Putin   **Arnolfini**

Sir,

Has anyone noticed the extraordinary similarity between President Putin of Russia and the bridegroom Signor Giovanni Arnolfini in the painting by Jan Van Eyck? Are they by any chance related?

ENA B. SEWELL,
Via Ena-mail.

Duchess   **Heseltine**

Sir,

I wonder whether your readers have noticed the extraordinary resemblance between Michael Heseltine and Princess Alice, Duchess of Gloucester. Are they by any chance related?

RICHARD CARRINGTON,
Minchinhampton, Gloucestershire.

Peel   **Padre**

Sir,

I was struck by the remarkable resemblance between the blessed Padre Pio and the almost eponymous John Peel of Radio 4 etc. Is there any relationship? I think we should be told.

DAVID J. ELLIS,
Burnley.

Sir,
I wonder if any of your readers have noticed, as I have, the strange resemblance between the signature of Osama bin Laden and a Kalashnikov. Surely they cannot be related in any way?
Yours,
ENA B. MADEUPNAME,
W1.

Orc   **Bowyer**

Sir,
Please find enclosed photographs of the mild-mannered association footballer, Lee Bowyer, and an unnamed actor from a recent Hollywood blockbuster. I was struck by the similarities between the two. Do you think they might be related?
Yours faithfully,
RONNIE JONES,
Coulsdon, Surrey.

Adams   **Mullah**

Sir,
Have your readers noticed the startling similarity between the Taliban ambassador to Pakistan, Mullah Abdul Salam Zaeef, and Gerry Adams Sinn Fein/IRA leader? Are they in any way genetically and ideologically related?
Yours perspicaciously,
RICHARD E. WILSON,
Rochford, Essex.

Morris   **Rattle**

Sir,
The enclosed photographs show, as I have long suspected, that Jan Morris is the pen name of the eminent conductor Sir Simon Rattle. Sir Simon is about to take over the Berlin Philharmonic Orchestra, an evening job which will leave no time for gadding about the globe writing travel books. Hence the recent decision of 'Jan Morris' to retire. I thought you ought to be told.
Yours faithfully,
MICHAEL KILGARRIFF,
London W5.

Fuzzy Fur Feet   **Johnson**

Sir,
I wonder if any of your other readers have noticed the astonishing similarity between Mr Boris Johnson MP and Fuzzy Fur Feet, from Dr Seuss's 'The Foot Book'? Do you think by any chance they might be related? I think we should be told.
Yours faithfully,
FRANK DANES,
Cambridge.

Letwin   **Colombo**

Sir,
Is the Independent on Saturday trying to kid us? Shouldn't the headline read "The famous dishevelled detective, Lieutenant Colombo..." Or is he under cover? "Oliver Letwin" – I don't believe it, sounds like a made-up name to me.
Yours,
VALERIE HILL,
Stroud, Glos.

Rimington   **Robinson**

Sir,
My spies inform me that Anne Robinson has been leading a secret double life as the head of MI5. Whose intelligence is sadly lacking? Whose licence to kill has a few too many points on it? Stella Rimington, you ARE the weakest agent – goodbye.
Yours,
PETER J. BLEACKLEY,
Littlehampton, Sussex.

Rushdie   **Next archbishop**

Sir,
I enclose a picture of the next Archbishop of Canterbury and one of Rowan Williams as well.
Yours,
PETER SMITH,
Newport, S. Wales.

Kahn   **Connery**

Sir,
I was struck by the resemblance between Ismail Kahn (legendary Iranian-backed leader, who escaped a Taliban jail in 1998) and Sir Sean Connery (who heroically escaped Alcatraz as part of his character preparation for "The Rock" with Nicholas Cage)... Might they be related?
Best regards,
JONATHAN BROWNE,
Japan.

Stanley   **David**

Sir,
I could not help but notice, when Mr David Beckham unveiled his new hair-do, what a striking resemblance he bears to Mr Stanley Laurel. Are they related?
TREVOR MARSHALL,
Via email.

Aziz   **Sellers**

Sir,
Has anyone noticed, I wonder, the striking resemblance between Iraqi Foreign Minister Tariq Aziz and the late Peter Sellers?
MARK,
Tribune, NW3.

The Post Office   **Consignia**

Sir,
Has anyone noticed the remarkable similarity between Consignia, the company formerly known as the Post Office, and Consignia, the company that is soon to be re-rebranded as the Royal Mail? Are they in any way not related?
Yours,
POSTMAN PAT,
Via snail mail.

(BLACK and white footage of grim Northern-style town with factory chimneys, men in cloth caps and street urchins playing hop-scotch on cobbled streets)

Narrator *(for it is some terrible actor)*: Britain in the post-war years was a very black and austere place. The war had left the country bankrupt and exhausted. The average wage was 18/6 a week in old money and most families could barely afford to eat.

(Shot of very old man wearing yellow socks sitting in armchair in London club)

Lord Deedes *(for it is he)*: Everyone sheemsh to forget that there wash shtill cheeshe rationing in 1953. You were only allowed half an ounce of cheeshe a week, per pershon. Thatsh not a lot of cheeshe, if you're fond of cheeshe, which I am.

(Old newsreel footage of women in headscarves queueing outside shop with notice reading "SORRY NO CHEESE TODAY")

Pathé-type Commentator: Housewives queued in vain all over Britain as cheese deliveries from America failed to materialise. So for the ladies, it was a case of "hard cheese"!

But never mind, soon the King will be dead and we can have a Coronation to cheer us all up!

Narrator: Then in February 1952 came the grim news.

(Shot of black-edged news placard reading "THE KING IS DEAD". Cut to man in pin-striped suit sitting in agreeable book-lined study)

Lord Bore *(Constitutional expert)*: The extraordinary thing about the British constitution is that the very moment a monarch dies, in this case the late King, at that very second his heir becomes King, or in this case Queen. Just like that! In the twinkling of an eye! Amazing! Just imagine, she went to bed a Princess and, sometime in the night, she mysteriously became the Queen! Could I have my fee in cash, please? Spot of bother with the wine merchant, you understand.

Narrator: But it wasn't all fun and games! Sorry, I'll do that bit again. It wasn't all doom and gloom! Suddenly the dark clouds parted, and a dazzling ray of sunshine lit up the bleak landscape of post-war, austerity-shrouded... oh no, I've done that bit. Suddenly Britain had a new young Queen and everyone agreed that it was the dawn of a new Elizabethan age.

What You Missed

1953
THE WAY WE WERE
—— *(as seen on all TV channels)* ——

(Cut to extremely dull-looking academic in library)

Ben Pimlott *(for it is he)*: It was the dawn of a new Elizabethan age. The dark clouds of post-war austerity rolled away, and suddenly there was something to cheer about.

(Black and white footage of Coronation. Golden coach, radiant Queen, Westminster Abbey, Peers in robes, Zadok the Priest, you know the stuff. Posh woman in chintzy drawing room with dogs)

Lady Pamela Ghastly *(for it is she)*: The Coronation was the most tremendous fun. We all had to get up terribly early, to be at the Abbey by half-past five. And you couldn't go to the loo, even if you were bursting. Some of the peers got frightfully hungry and began to eat their coronets. It was frightfully funny. And then, when we got home, we found all our servants and estate workers had been watching the whole thing on a little television set which we'd bought specially for them. They'd enjoyed it all so much. And, you know, one of them had been waving at us all day, thinking that we could see him! Ha, ha, ha!

Narrator: But it wasn't just the gentry who were able to join in the fun. All along the route of the Coronation procession that June morning were millions of loyal subjects waiting to catch a glimpse of their radiant young Queen. Many of them had been camping out for a week.

(Cut to woman in Old People's Home, surrounded by Coronation mugs, Union Jacks and pictures of Enoch Powell)

Mrs Doris Stothard *(for it is she)*: We all camped out for a week. I had my two little girls with me. But the youngest, Sylvia, got lost in the crowd when she went to find the toilet. But then a kind policeman brought her back, safe and sound. And I said to him...

Voice of Producer: Can you forget the policeman and get back to how it started raining and it didn't dampen your spirits?

Mrs Stothard: Oh yes... it started to rain but it didn't dampen our spirits. And we were all very excited when we heard that they'd climbed Mount Everest. Is that right?

(Jerky black and white footage of two men sitting outside tent on snow-covered mountain. Caption: Edmund Hillary And Sherpa Howard Resting At Base Camp After Their Historic Climb. Posh woman in room with even more dogs)

Lady Pamela: We were all so proud. Of course, Mr Hillary came from New Zealand. But in those days we thought of him as an Englishman. And the same goes for the little Sherpa, even though he was coloured! Ha, ha, ha!

(Cut back to woman in Old People's Home)

Mrs Stothard: As I was saying, it started to rain, but in no way did it dampen our spirits. And there was a great cheer when this big black lady went past in a coach. "That's Winifred Atwell," said my husband. And, d'you know, it was!

Voice of Producer: No, no, no... For heaven's sake, Mrs Stothard, it was the Queen of bloody Tonga. How many times do I have to tell you?

(Black and white footage of Winifred Atwell playing black and white rag)

Narrator: And then came the very best news of all. It was announced that cheese rationing had come to an end!

(Cut to technicolour archive film showing young William Deedes [aged 63] eating cheese sandwich at East End street party and giving cheery thumbs-up sign to camera)

Pathé-style Commentator: A perfect end to a perfect day! Thank you, Ma'am, and God bless you! As the song has it, "It's summertime and the living is cheesy!"

(Music over: Billy Cotton and his orchestra play 'Zadok The Priest')

A BBC12 Co-Production With Television Romania and WT-XCJ Ontario

HIGHGROVE PARK

PG

AN old-fashioned lavish country house drama where a group of ill-assorted aristocrats, nouveaux riches and showbiz types gather for a weekend at the invitation of their host, the eccentric Prince Charles with his mistress Camilla Parker Bowles.

Among the weekend guests are a famous poet (Andrew Motion), an obscure novelist (Robert Harris), a pianist and crooner (Jools Holland) and an elderly peeress (Dame Helena Kennedy).

Why have they all gathered together? What secrets lurk beneath their civilised exteriors?

The rich comedy turns to tragedy when all the guests are found bored to death in the library. The murder weapon seems to be an old record of the Goon show still playing on the desk.

Inspector Knacker (Stephen Fry) is confronted by one of the most baffling mysteries of his career.

Why have all these people accepted an invitation from Prince Charles?

——— Cast In Full ———

PRINCE CHARLES	Michael Gambon
CAMILLA PARKER BOWLES	Dame Judi Dench
ANDREW MOTION	Charles Dance
JOOLS HOLLAND	Ivor Novello
DAME HELENA KENNEDY	Maggie Smith
ROBERT HARRIS	Alan Bates

(That's enough cast. Ed.)

NOW SHOWING AT THE FOLLOWING GNOMEONS

■ **GOSFORD PARK** ■ **WIDDECOMBE FAIR**
■ **WOODHEAD** ■ **MANDELSON WEST**
■ **EDWARD HEATH** ■ **ARDENT END**

(That's enough cinemas).

Four paces behind, woman

Aren't you taking this Islamic thing a bit far, Charles?

Your Cut Out 'n' Keep Guide To The Queen's Round-Britain Golden Jubilee Tour

May 1 The Queen will open the School of Contemporary Cake-making in Dundee.

May 4 The Queen will visit the new set of traffic lights in Nuneaton High Street.

May 21 The Queen will attend a performance of line-dancing given by pupils of the Abergavenny Junior School.

May 28 The Queen will open a new car-park at the Civic Centre, Keynsham.

May 30 The Queen will visit the Highland Moth Museum in Pitlochry.

June 4 The Queen will lay the foundation stone for the new Vodaphone warehouse at the Business Park.

June 14 The Queen will attend a luncheon for senior citizens at the McDonald's Restaurant, Chorleywood.

June 23 The Queen will "cut the first sod" of the A7598 extension to the Morpeth by-pass, Northumberland.

July 6 The Queen will take a tram ride on the new Wakefield Metrolink.

July 14 The Queen will unveil a plaque to mark the birthplace of Ronnie Corbett in Potters Bar.

July 20 The Queen will be mugged on a visit to Brixton in South London, and will have her mobile telephone removed. *(Surely some mistake? Ed.)*

THE REAL GYLES BRANDRETH

by Her Majesty The Queen

IN A unique opportunity, Her Majesty The Queen has been allowed special access to Gyles Brandreth as he goes about his duties trying to fill space in the Sunday Telegraph. Read her amazing insight, starting today.

Tuesday 4th October

Today, Gyles is due to open a paragraph, but he can obviously think of nothing to say. One is surprised that after all these years of appearing in public he canot come up with a few words!

Wednesday 7th October

Gyles has granted an audience to his editor, Sir Dominic Lawson. Lawson asks politely how his latest piece is going.

Brandreth doesn't seem to know who Lawson is and walks past him without a word.

Later, he tells me, "One has to meet so many different people when one is doing this job."

Tomorrow: Gyles celebrates fifty glorious words about the Queen.

"Damn it, woman, how much moisturiser do you use?"

PARLIAMENTARY DEBATES

(Han-z-z-z-ard – sponsored by Mittal [Dutch Antilles] plc. Motto: "It's a Steel!")

3.17 pm. Trade & Industry Questions

Mrs Toreeza Nogood (Virginia Bottom, Con): Would the Secretary of State agree that, in the light of this truly disgraceful behaviour, he should jolly well resign?

(Tory cheers)

Iain Duncan Donuts (Wheen, Con): I say, jolly well said Theresa, cough, cough.

(Tory cheers and coughs)

Mr Stephen Lyers (Pants-On-Fire, Lab): I have no intention of resigning, now or at any other time. I have been told by the Prime Minister that I must apologise for any lies I may inadvertently have told, but I must make it clear that I have not told any, and, even if I had, so what? Let's stop all this asking silly questions about whether I've told lies or not, and get back to the real business of this government, which is banning fox-hunting.

(Labour cheers)

Mrs Nogood: Is there *anything* that will make you resign, you horrid man?

Mr John Prescott (Two Jags, Lab): Shut yer bloody face, yer fat slag!

(Hysterical Labour cheers and laughter at this outstanding example of modern parliamentary wit)

The Speaker (Mr Mick Gorbals): Och aye, yer bloody Tory houri, John's richt the nicht.

(Labour cheers and laughter at this outstanding example of parliamentary impartiality by Mr McSpeaker)

Charles Wannabe (Glenfiddich, Lib-Dem): Would the Secretary of State agree that, in the light of his truly disgraceful behaviour, he should jolly well resign?

Mrs Nobody: Hey, that's what I said!

(Lib-Dem cheers, Labour boos, Tory coughs)

Mr Lyers: Run, run, as fast as you can. You can't catch me, I'm Tony's man!

(Labour erupts in spontaneous demonstration of support for Mr Lyers's superb handling of all problems affecting Britain's transport system)

Mr Norman Baker (Boring-on-Thames, Lib-Dem): Can I ask the Prime Minister...

Mr J. Prescott: No, you bloody well can't, because he's not here.

(House adjourns for weekend, since it is Tuesday)

NEW BBC SERIES
Yes, F****** Minister

(Scene: The minister's private office at the Department of Transport. Door opens, and Sir Humphrey enters.)

Sir Humphrey Mottram: Good f****** morning, minister.

Minister: What the f*** do you want?

Sir Humphrey: We're f****** f*****, minister.

Minister: You mean to say we're f****** f*****?

Sir Humphrey: Yes, f****** minister.

Minister: F*** me!

Ends

CAST IN FULL

SIR RICHARD MOTTRAM	**Ali G.**
THE MINISTER	**Stephen Fryers**
MARTIN SIXSMITH	**Himself**
JO MOORE	**Barbara Windsor**

Produced by Quentin Tarantino

"What are you doing here? You've been made redundant – didn't you get the letter...?"

BYERS: NEW LIE

> I do not look silly in this hat

OLD WOMAN DEMANDS 'RIGHT TO LIVE'

by Our Medical Staff **Hugh Thanasia**

IN AN extraordinary legal case currently being heard in London, an old woman, described as "terminally washed-up", yesterday pleaded that she be allowed to "live with dignity".

The woman, known to the court only as "Mrs T", told the judge that although she could no longer make speeches, she could still communicate with the outside world thanks to the miracle of issuing regular statements to the media to whom she is connected 24 hours a day.

HOPELESS

But an independent medical expert, Dr Iain Duncan Smith, pleaded that the woman's life-support system be turned off at once.

"She has led a very full life," he said, "but she no longer has anything useful to contribute, particularly on the subject of Europe or anything else.

"The really compassionate course," Dr Duncan Stoat continued, "would be to turn her off and put us out of our misery."

TIDE TURNS IN FAVOUR OF NEW-LOOK TORIES

by Our Political Staff **Janet Daley-Telegraph**

MAKE no mistake. The signs are now multiplying in all directions that the Tory Party is on the brink of a massive breakthrough under its quietly dynamic new leader Ian Duncan Cough.

Though admittedly no orator, and totally lacking in charisma, Duncan Cough has in the past six months stamped his feet *(surely "his personal authority on the party"? Ed)* and redefined what it means to be a Conservative in the 21st century *(Keep going, this is perfect. C.M.)*.

In his mould-breaking speech to dozens of cheering supporters at Harrogate, Duncan Cough said: "Our party has always been the party of the poor, the disabled, the working man and the ethnic minorities.

"If Conservatism means anything it means an attack on the privileged classes with their top hats, their fox hunting and their public school mentality."

No wonder his words have galvanised the ranks of the Tory faithful as never before.

As one grass-roots activist told me after the speech, "I think I've come to the wrong conference."

YOU choose the new name for the caring, compassionate Tory Party

1. **Conservia**
....
2. **Accentory**
....
3. **Parcel Force**
....
4. **Coughs 'Я' Us**
....
5. **The Labour Party**
....

☎ Ring this number now and tell us what you think.

08987 42357 4218

All calls will be charged at premium rate and all profits will be used to build day care centres for gay toddlers.

NEW-LOOK TORIES

We're going to shed our Victor Meldrew image

I don't bel-*ieve* it!!

'Macabre Horror Show' Goes Ahead

by Our Arts Staff **BRIAN R. SEWELL**

A CONTROVERSIAL exhibition of dead bodies has been put on public display in Harrogate under the title "The Conservative Party".

Originally created by the sinister Dr Keith Joseph in the 1970s, the exhibition features the lifeless torsos of dozens of members of the Conservative Party who have volunteered to donate their bodies to the project.

Nobodyworlds

Critics have called the exhibition "a disgusting and morbid spectacle appealing only to ghouls", but the organisers are defiant.

One Plastination Tories

"These people may be dead but they perform an educational role for young people today who want to discover how people get frozen in time."

The organisers claim that the anonymous corpses are now extremely popular and that the exhibition will be moving on to Westminster shortly.

Iain Duncan Stiff is 73.

WHY I WON'T BE TALKING ABOUT MY CHILDREN

by **Iain Duncan Smith**

UNLIKE Tony Blair, you won't catch me mentioning my children. Oh no. You probably didn't know I had any until I just mentioned them. Well I do. But I am not going to talk about them because I don't want to exploit them for political purposes. I'll leave that to Labour's Tony Blair!

By not mentioning them I think I'm being a rather better father and all-round family man than some other people I could mention, i.e. Euan Blair's Dad!

So when it comes to the election do remember the candidate who doesn't harp on about his children all the time – even though he has lots of them and could fill up whole books about how brilliant and talented they all are. But I choose not to discuss them at all.
© *Iain Duncan Donutz*

On Other Pages

Those unknown children in full **2-9**

GAY COPPER SHOCK

"Hello, hello, hello, sailor"

 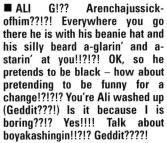

GLENDA SLAGG

FLEET STREET'S WMD – WOMAN OF MASS DESTRUCTION!

■ ALI G!?? Arenchajussick-ofhim??!?! Everywhere you go there he is with his beanie hat and his silly beard a-glarin' and a-starin' at you!!?!?! OK, so he pretends to be black – how about pretending to be funny for a change!?!?!? You're Ali washed up (Geddit???!) Is it because I is boring??!? Yes!!!! Talk about boyakashingin!!?!? Geddit????!

■ BEANIE HATS off to Ali G?!?! He's the funniest man in da hood, as we say in the Fleet Street massive!!?!?! Respect, Ali?? You've got mine!!?! I'd like to be your Julie, make no da mistake!!!? Chillin', blink blink rappin' Shaggy... er... (That's enough da. Ed.)

■ DIDYA shed a tear at li'l Liza Minnelli's all-star wedding in romantic downtown Ground Zero??!? I did, Mister, and I'm not ashamed to say so!!!?!

Fourth time lucky, Liza, cos, as the song says, life is like a cabaret, and yours is still the best in town!!!?! You're an icon to us all, just like your Mum – altogether now, "Somewhere over the rainbow..."

■ I CRIED at ludicrous Liza's wedding – with laughter!!?!?! Roll up, roll up for the freak show starring Michael Jackson as the Zombie and Elizabeth Taylor as the Fat Lady!!?!?! Check the spelling Mr Sub-Editor – it's Liza with a z-z-z-z!!! (Geddit???!?)

PS. See you at the Divorce Court, Liza. All together now, "We're off to see the lawyers..."

■ *COMMANDER PADDICK?!!?!!? Donchajuslovehim? Here's a copper who is glad to be gay and smokes the odd joint – just like we all do in this day and age!!! No wonder the carping killjoys and the moaning Middle Englanders want to see him strung up!!??!? Good luck, Commander – and keep on a-puffin' and a-poofin' all round London!!!!? You're a fair cop!!?!? (Geddit???!)*

■ COMMANDER PADDICK?!!??! Arenchasickofhim???! What a disgrace!!?!? No wonder crime is out of control when Brixton's boys in blue are a-cruisin' and a-woozin' around the back street!!?!?! Shame Commander!!??!?? If ever there was a bent copper it's you??!? Geddit???!?? So get off the beat and take up hairdressing!?!?!?!

HERE they are, Glenda's Easter Honey Bunnies!!!?!

● **Peter Wilby** – He's the dreamy editor of the New Statesman!!! Yu can stagger round to my place, Peter, and see my circulation rise!?!???

● **Lakshmi Mittal** – Come and show me what your steel is made of – and you don't have to give me any money!!!!?!!

● **Chris Woodhead** – I know I'm a bit old for you, but you can teach me some lessons anytime!??!?!

Byeeee!!!

"Then, of course, there's the overtime, the red tape and the ridiculous cost of housing, not to mention backache from all the sitting around..."

POLICE COMPLAINTS AUTHORITY

N.U.T. STRIKE OVER TEACHER SHORTAGES

by our Education Staff **Polly Technic**

MR DAVID SPART, the Assistant Vice Chair of the National Union of Teaching Operatives (Lambeth Branch) last night confirmed that his members would be taking strike action over the coming weeks.

However he warned that due to staff shortages, supply teachers would have to be brought in to go on strike.

Agitation, Agitation, Agitation

"There are not nearly enough trained teachers to cover all the picket lines," he said, "and it is a total tragedy that there are insufficient numbers of teachers to not teach our children."

NEWS IN BRIEF

POPE ADMITS: THERE MAY BE PAEDOPHILES IN THE PRIESTHOOD

POPE ADMITS: 'YES, I MAY BE A CATHOLIC'

BEAR ADMITS: 'OK, ON SOME OCCASIONS I MAY HAVE SHAT IN THE WOODS'

TV Highlights

Father Ped
(UK Gold)

CLASSIC last episode in which Father Ped is excommunicated by the Pope for "sins against humanity".

CAST IN FULL

Father Ped . . . . . . P.D. O'Phile
The Pope . . . . . Marlon Brando
Man in prison . . . . Lord Archer
Next week: *Auf Wiedersehen, Ped*

Eye Rating: Urgh....

48

Never Too Old...

by Dame Sylvie Krin

THE STORY SO FAR: The lovely Wendy Deng has persuaded her husband, the ageing media tycoon Rupert Murdoch, to accompany her to the world's most glamorous awards ceremony, the Oscars. Now read on...

"AND the award for the Best Assistant Make-Up Artist on a foreign language film goes to..."

"Jeez, Wendy!" barked the septuagenarian Australian mogul. "How many more of these flamin' pooftahs are we gonna have to watch picking up their gongs from that abo woman on the stage?"

"Shush, Lupert," his wife admonished him, placing a bread roll in his mouth. "Evelyone listening!"

Rupert slumped back in his chair and tried to loosen his bowtie. It had been a mistake to drink so many bottles of the Santa Monica Lewinsky Californian Chardonnay before taking their seats. They had been in the vast room for 5 hours and it felt like 50. Still, it would soon be over. And with any luck he could be tucked up in bed reading the company accounts from his global empire before midnight.

But his comforting reverie was interrupted by the strains of the Hollywood Bowl Symphony Orchestra playing a tribute to the victims of 9/11, specially composed by Marty Snorheim, who wrote the award-winning score for the action thriller "The Mutant Chainsaw Death Massacre".

"Isn't this exciting, Lupert?" exclaimed Wendy, as her apricot petal lips broadened into a seductive oriental smile. "And we're only halfway through the awards."

"Christ! But *then* can we go home? I'm as pooped as a kookaburra who's lost his donger up a eucalyptus tree."

"No! No! Lupert! Then we go dancing! Party time for you, Lupert. Twist the night away at Vanity Fair..."

"VANITY Fair? Certainly Mr Murdoch. Do come in." The portly figure of the world's most famous magazine editor, Graydon Carshole III, extended a limp hand.

"May I introduce you to Hymie Schotzenberger and his wife Guantanamera? Also Mrs Tutzi von Bulow and her friend Pinky Wagstaffe?"

Although the lovely Wendy was in her element in the glitzy crowd at Moron's Restaurant, spotting the stars and chatting with the younger celebrities, Rupert was ill at ease.

His fashionable open-neck shirt, which Wendy had insisted he wore instead of his tuxedo, made him feel uncomfortable.

"Is your father alright?" asked Mrs Jerome Wildebeest, the celebrated Hollywood columnist, offering Wendy a glass of water.

"It's very good of you to have brought him. It's so good for old people to get out and about and meet some new faces. I've brought my mother. She's asleep in a chair over there next to Dame Judi Dench. Shall I take him over for you?

"Come on, dear," she shrilled into the ear of the owner of the Times newspaper. "We'll let your daughter go off now and find some young nice man to dance with."

"No, no, no," interjected the exotic temptress from the land of bird's nest soup, "Lupert dance with me. Until he drop!"

Wendy was as good as her word and, snatching him away from the astonished gaze of Mrs Wildebeest, she dragged him onto the dance floor, where a raucous band were about to launch into a frenzied rap version of the theme from the movie Titanic.

"Women and children first!" she cried excitedly. "Old men go down with ship. Ha, ha, ha!"

Rupert, overcome with nausea and fatigue, gasped for breath as the waves seemed to close over his head... *(To be continued)*

OSCAR SHOCK!

You see? Black actresses can make really embarrassing speeches as well...

Late News

DAME JUDI *NOT* IN FILM

– PUBLIC OUTRAGED

A MAJOR film was released yesterday not featuring Dame Judi Dench. The producers apologised and promised it would not happen again.

(Reuters)

PRE-SCHOOL NURSERY RHYMES

There was an old woman who lived in a shoe,
She wanted some decent affordable accommodation in London –
So what else could she do?

POLLY FILLER

Not Columnist of the Year 2002

I AM proud to announce to my readers that I did *not* win anything at all at this year's B&Q/Kwik-Fit UK National and Regional Press Awards – and I would like to thank all the judges who did not vote for me.

Because this year's awards were a FARCE – and all the winners should feel thoroughly ashamed of themselves.

Let us take one category at random – Woman Columnist Writing about Being At Home With Young Children (Broadsheets). It was clear to all of us at the dinner that the judges in this category (mostly failed journalists who couldn't get a gardening column in their local freesheet!) had decided that it was Ms Buggins' turn, and awarded it accordingly. Everybody cheered (ironically of course) when the bimbo in question (no names, but think bottle-blonde!!) went up to accept her tacky piece of fibreglass. And when they read out her column about the day her au pair put the hamster in the washing machine, the audience all laughed (but *at* her rather than with her! Sad really!).

EVERYONE who I spoke to agreed that the award *should* have gone to the journalist who had written the touching account of how her life had changed for ever on 9/11. The way she had explained the tragedy to her wide-eyed toddler Charlie (Bless!) and tried to get her useless partner Simon to turn over to CNN for the news (and stop watching Pro-Celebrity Salad-Tossing from the Maldives presented by Paul Ross) was almost unbearably moving. In fact, a lot of people said they couldn't bear to read it.

So let's hear no more about these discredited awards because no one is interested in the meaningless ritual backslapping that so demeans our profession.

© Polly Filler. Winner of the DynoRod/Stannah Stair Lift Lifestyle Journalism Award 1987

JURY FINDS R.E.M. MAN 'FAMOUS'

by Our Celebrity Staff **Donna Air Rage**

MR PETER BUCK, the guitarist with the popular singing group R.E.M. was yesterday found by a jury to be "Extremely Famous" and therefore not guilty of anything at all.

The court had been presented with conclusive evidence of Mr Buck's celebrity – including a testimonial from the legendary Irish expert witness Mr "Bono" Bono.

Despite a number of unfamous witnesses saying that Mr Buck was disgracefully drunk on red wine during a flight and had behaved appallingly towards the cabin crew, the jury were swayed by the revelation that Mr Buck had sold lots of records and had been on the telly.

The Buck Doesn't Stop Here

A relieved Mr Buck said, "I am delighted with this result. It proves once and for all that nobody is above the law unless they are famous."

Those R.E.M. Hits In Full

1. **The Drinks Trolley**
2. **The Stewardess**
3. **The Captain**

WHY LOOK MR MAYOR, HE WANTS TO SHAKE YOUR HAND

FREEMASON WILLY

CHERIE MEETS YOKO

You're only famous because of who your husband is

A Doctor Writes

How vaccines work

WHAT happens is that the businessman injects a small amount of cash into the body politic or *Corpus blairus nulaborensis*, to give it the full medical title.

In a very short time the businessman is covered in a huge rash of money which will ensure that his bank balance remains healthy for years (or as long as he remembers to "top up" his injections).

There are, however, occasional side effects, including the possibility of outbreaks of unwelcome publicity *(Sleazus tabloidus exposensis)*. But there is no cause for alarm and after a few days the symptoms will disappear.

If you are worried about your business, give Tony Blair some money.

© A Doctor.

Births

TO ELIZABETH HURLEY, a million pound baby boy, Damian. Mother and cheque are well and Damian is said to have his mother's eyes and his father's money. Flowers should be sent c/o Elton John.

Those Hurley Names In Full

At last Private Eye can reveal the complete shortlist of names that Liz drew up before selecting Damian.

666	**Salem**
Dracula	**Adolf**
Frankenstein	**Judas**
Beelzebub	**Peregrine Worsthorne**

AND STILL THEY COME

by our Royal Staff PHIL PAPER

IT IS nearly two weeks since the Queen Mother died yet hundreds and thousands of articles are still filing into the newspapers. Long and short, old and thin, the articles come in all shapes and sizes and stretch from the front page all the way to the crossword – but they all share the same emotion. Desperation.

Some pieces have appeared two or three times and yet they are still queuing up to be published again.

River Of Guff

There has been a huge tide of sadness engulfing the nation's journalists who feel that this is their last chance to sell a piece about the Queen Mother. "We shall not see the like of these pieces again," said one tearful journalist. "It's the end of an era. An era in which you could file any old rubbish about the Royal Family and it would go straight in."

Amongst those slowly moving their hands across the keyboard in silent tribute were such household names as John Mortimer, Melanie Phillips, A.N. Wilson, Hugo Young, Andrew Roberts, Ingrid Sewage and the late Bill Deedes.

Only the stony-hearted could have failed to be moved to tears by the spectacle of these hacks churning out millions of words to *(cont. p.94)*

AN APOLOGY
Mr Jon Snow And The Channel Four News Team

IN OUR broadcast just before the funeral ceremonies for the late Queen Mother, we may have given the impression that the monarchy was entirely washed up and no longer of any interest to the British public. Vox pop interviews like that with Miss Tanya Lymeswold outside the King's Lynn Waitrose, in which she said "no, they're irrelevant really, these days people are more interested in the Lottery and Big Brother", may have reinforced this impression. Mr Snow's concluding prediction that "the Queen's Mother's funeral will be the biggest switch-off in TV history" and will "undoubtedly mark the end of the monarchy as we know it" may have led viewers to believe that Channel Four regarded the death of the late Queen as a trivial and unimportant event to which we would be giving no further coverage.

We now realise that the Queen Mother was a towering historical figure whose death was possibly the most important event of the entire century, which has done more than anything to reinforce the natural loyalty of the British people to the monarchy. As Mrs Ludmilla Nargs so eloquently put it in one of our many special broadcasts on the Lying-in-State, "She was our history. She was everything that Britain stands for. I am totally gutted."

We apologise for any confusion which may have arisen from our earlier reports, and can only plead in mitigation that all the other channels were just as bad.

Letters to the Editor

The Queen Mother

SIR – Surely those who were responsible for the magnificent, split-second organisation of the Royal Funeral should be appointed to run Railtrack without delay (and perhaps air traffic control into the bargain!).
NRP Ghastly
Haywards Heath

SIR – I once had the great honour to meet Her Late Majesty Queen Elizabeth the Queen Mother, when she graciously attended the opening of the Monmouth Moth Museum in 1974. Her Majesty showed the greatest possible interest in all the moths on display (7) and joked that she hoped they would not eat her hat. Truly we shall not see her like again.
Rhodri Rees-Bore
Monmouth

SIR – The British people have once again shown their contempt for the Guardian-eating, muesli-wearing chattering classes who sneeringly forecast that no one would bother to turn up for the Queen Mother's Funeral.
So much for 'Cool Britannia'!
Yours sincerely
R.D. Smythe-Smythe
(Col. Retired)
Weymouth

SIR – If they are looking for a new Queen Mother, there can surely be only one candidate – Sir Elton John.
Mike Giggler
Via e-mail

Letters

The Queen Mother

Have I been on another planet, or has something important happened? An old lady has died aged 101. Hundreds of them do every day, but I don't notice the Guardian putting them on the front page. Can we have a sense of proportion please?
Keith Stiggles
Hackney

● It is sickening that, at a time when the world is teetering on the brink of a nuclear holocaust started by the Fascist Bush and his poodle Blair, that the media should be literally inundated with sickening drivel about some outdated relic of the parasitic feudal class, i.e. the so-called Queen Mother, a known sympathiser with Hitler in 1940 and, er…
Yours faithfully
The Hon. Rupert Twistleton-Spart
Ascot

● The cost of the funeral of the Queen Mother has been reliably estimated by the New Spartsman at £6.3 billion. This would be enough to build 823 new hospitals or 378 schools, or to provide 24-hour child care for every working woman in the whole country. Need I say more?
Mrs Ludmilla Rusbridger
Chorleywood

● Who is now to replace the Queen Mother in the nation's affections? I would suggest Sir Elton John.
Mike Giggler
Via e-mail

TOP ROYALS FLY IN TO PAY LAST RESPECTS

BY OUR ROYAL STAFF PHILLIPA PAGE

HUNDREDS of the world's top Royals flew in yesterday to pay their last respects to Her Majesty Queen Elizabeth the Queen Mother.

Not since the funeral of Queen Victoria in 1901 had so many of the world's top Royals flown in to pay their last respects to the woman they called simply Her Majesty Queen Elizabeth the Queen Mother.

Who were they, these top Royals who flew in to pay their last respects to Her Majesty Queen Elizabeth the Queen Mother?

Private Eye is proud to present this unique cut-out-and-keep guide to the top Royals who flew in to pay their last respects to the Queen Mother.

"She was the Queen of Hats…"

Princess Vanilla of Haagen-Dazs

Ex-King Boris of Johnson and Queen Petronella of Wyfrontia

The Tandoori of Hinduja

His Highness the Count Oranjeboom of Holsten-Pils

His Royal Highness the Archduke Heineken of Carlsberg

Her Royal Highness the Queen Camilla of Uganda
(Surely some mistake? Ed.)

The Daily Telegraph

A Special Editorial by Sir Charles Moore O.E., Editor of the Daily Telegraph

If there is one message which has come out loud and clear from the momentous events which have attended the obsequies of Her Majesty Queen Elizabeth the Queen Mother, it is that the whole nation is united in contempt for Mr Blair and his New Labour government. As I left the Abbey after that incomparably moving funeral service, on every side there was only one topic of conversation. Why had the Prime Minister not worn proper morning dress for the occasion, unlike Mr Iain Duncan Smith or indeed myself? Mr Blair is, of course, a busy man. But surely the very least he could have done was to put aside half-an-hour to pay a visit to Moss Bros, or perhaps borrow some proper clothes from an Old Etonian friend.

As for the Prime Minister's wife, the less said about her the better. With her frightful hat and ghastly dress, swinging her handbag in an inappropriately jaunty manner, she looked exactly like one of those awful model-girls we have on almost every page of the Telegraph these days.

But at least for one thing we can all be truly grateful. We did not have to endure the spectacle of Mr Blair reading the lesson, as we did five years ago at the funeral of the late Diana, Princess of Wales.

Nor was there any of that dreadful caterwauling from that man in a wig.

No. On all sides the congregation were agreed. New Labour is finished. As the Archbishop of Canterbury so eloquently put it in his excellent sermon, speaking for the entire nation, "Strength, dignity and laughter. Iain Duncan Smith has them all. Vote Conservative."

© *The Daily Tailorgraph and Morning Dress.*

By popular request, the Daily Telegraph is reprinting what was universally agreed to be the highlight of the Funeral Service, the recitation of the styles and titles of the late Queen Mother by the Garter King-At-Arms, Major General Sir Roderick Voletrouser G.C.S.E.

"Her Imperial and Serene Majesty the Queen Elizabeth the Queen Mother, Dowager Empress of the Seven Seas, Dame Knight Cross of the Most Royal Order of the Thistle, Most Noble Lady of the Order of the Hot Cross Bun, Dame Commander of the Most High Order of the Imperial Leather, Most Puissante Relict of the Grand Wizard of the Raspberry, Colonel-in-Chief of the Queen's Own Highland Terriers, the Irish Boozaliers and 437 other regiments, Grand Mistress of the Worshipful Company of Tipplers and Distillers *(cont. pp 94-106)*

BATTLE OF BRITAIN MEMORIAL FLIGHT SURPRISES PRINCESS MICHAEL

Achtung! Spitfeuer!

Classical Brit Awards – Results In Full

Fiddler of the Year M. Fayed

Trumpet Blower (own) of the Year M. Fugger

Horn M. Fuggit

Passport Anglais Not awarded to M. Fugwit

Tenner of the Year The one slipped in the programme so that Mr Fuggoff could appear on television. *(That's enough Awards. Ed.)*

GLENDA SLAGG

THE GAL YOU WANT TO SHAG!!!
(Surely Not? Ed.)

■ **HATS OFF** to Nigella Lawson – the glamorous TV cook who is not ashamed to show off what she's REAR-ly made of!!?! Geddit???!? She's pure CL-ASS!!!? Geddit??!? Which one of us gals wouldn't die for a beautiful B-U-M like Nigella's!!?!? That's the Bottom Line Mister!!?! (Geddit??????!)

■ NIGELLA LAWSON – arencha-sickofher???! If she's not on the telly a-gobblin' and a-wobblin', there she is paradin' her bum like a tart – and I don't mean one she made earlier!!?! Geddit??!?! Take a tip from Glenda, Nigella love – if I had a rear end the size of yours, I'd park it in an aeroplane hangar and call it a day!!?! No offence!!!?

Byeeee!!!

"You'll have to go by yourself – I've no shoes"

THE BOOK OF SHARON

Chapter 94 – The Feast Of The Peace-over

1. And lo, it came to pass that the rulers of the Arab-ites took counsel amongst themselves, saying "Let us journey unto the city of Bei-rut, that we may talk of how to bring peace between the Araf-ites and the children of Israel."

2. "Though, to be frank, we cannot see much hope in it ourselves."

3. "And let us therefore call our brother Ara-fat, even he that weareth the towel upon his head, and summon him to Bei-rut to take counsel with us."

4. But Ara-fat was be-seiged in his tent in the place that is called Ram-allah, which is to say "the hole of hell".

5. And all around the tent of Ara-fat was camped a mighty host of Israelites, even with their chariots of fire.

6. For Sharon, that ruleth the children of Israel (at time of this Testament going to press), had decreed that Ara-fat must remain a prisoner within his tent, even as the desert fox must remain in his lair when the dogs seek him out to devour him.

7. But then a brilliant idea cometh to Sharon, as in a dream. "Why do I not letteth mine enemy, even Ara-fat, depart in peace from the land of Is-rael, to go to Bei-rut?"

8. "And, then, nudgeth, nudgeth, winketh, winketh, we decide that it cannot be safe to allow him to return."

9. "In this wise, he will have to remaineth in Bei-rut, which is a very dangerous place, if thou knowest what I mean?"

10. So Sharon rose up and sendeth unto Ara-fat, "Go forth, even to Bei-rut. For I will not stand in thy way, nor the children of Is-rael likewise."

11. But Ara-fat smelleth an rat, and sayeth unto Sharon, "I did not get where I am today by falling for that old trick."

12. So Ara-fat abideth where he was, even in Ram-allah. And thus the threat of peace passed from the land of Is-rael, which is why it was called from that time forth the feast of the Peace-over.

OLD JOKES REVISITED

I want to talk about peace

Peace off!

In Today's Telavivagraph

● Barbara Amiel Sharon on 'Why the Palestinians should be driven into the sea'.

● Unfunny cartoon by Hack to illustrate piece by the proprietor's wife.

© *Daily Telavivagraph*

A Taxi Driver writes

Every week a well-known Professor of Poetry is asked to make a fool of himself on an issue of topical importance.

THIS WEEK: **Tom Paulin** (Cab No. 666) on the crisis in the Middle East.

...Do you know who I blame guv for all that out there? Them bloody Jews – you know the American ones – blimey! What a load of Nazis!!! Tell you what I'd do with the Yankee Yids – I'd string 'em up. It's the only language they understand. I mean, people go on about Hitler but he had a point, didn't he – I mean, if there weren't all those Jews out in Israel then there wouldn't be no trouble.

I had that David Irving in the back of the cab – a very clever man.

'Ere, do you want a signed book of my latest poems? No? You a Jew or what?

Next week: Melanie 'Daily Mel' Phillips (Cab No. 7842) – "Why Blair's latest idea is terrible, whatever it is".

"Ah, look... his last steps"

54

BLAIR SPELLS IT OUT

We need peace in the Middle East, except in Iraq where we need war

---

Pret-a-Manger Square – Loaves and fishes to take away
Sorry – Closed

Bethlehem Star

AD1

HEROD DENIES MASSACRE OF INNOCENTS
by Jenin di Giovanni

KING ARIEL Herod, the Holy Land's Mr Big, today issued a categorical denial that there had been a massacre of hundreds of innocent children in and around the Bethlehem area.

Said Herod, 76, "We have been carrying out a defensive action codenamed 'Operation Slaughter', in order to stabilise the situation in Bethlehem."

He continued, "Troublemakers

Herod: "I deeply regret any unfortunate civilian casualties"

have been using a number of firstborn as human shields, making it sadly necessary for our forces to destroy the entire juvenile population of the time."

Reporters from the Bible have been banned, "purely for their own safety," according to the head of Operation Slaughter.

Meanwhile, the so-called Three Wise Men who were on a peace mission to the region have called off their proposed meeting with Herod due to a last-minute dream.

● *Your camel trains tonight* **7**

Today Programme

Naughtie *(for it is he)*:
...thanks very much indeed, Ambassador. And now the terrible news, just breaking, about that woman's body which has been found in the Thames. Obviously it's far too early to say for certain that it's the missing schoolgirl Millie, but inevitably there will be speculation that it is indeed the missing teenager, and at such a time it's only natural for us to try to imagine what it must be like for Millie's parents as they sit there waiting for the moment they've dreaded – the moment when they are told that the body in the Thames is that of their daughter. Although, of course, I must emphasise that at the moment we don't yet know for certain that it is Millie. We have on the line someone who can talk us through what it is like for any parent to have to face what is surely any parent's worst nightmare, the chair of the National Association of Grief Councillors...
(The programme continues in similar tasteless vein for several minutes until news bulletin reveals that the body is not that of Millie after all)

THAT SHARON U.N. COMMISSION
How It Will Look

THE Prime Minister of Israel has submitted to the United Nations the names of observers whom he considers to have "suitable expertise" to form "a sensible judgement" on recent events at the Jenin refugee camp.

The nominees are:
● **General Augusto Pinochet** (former Chilean statesman)
● **The late Dr Verwoerd** (former Prime Minister of the Republic of South Africa)
● **General Ariel Sharon** (no relation)

"Death to Israel, death to America, death to Britain. Until tomorrow, this is Ali Mohamed wishing you a pleasant evening"

OWZAT!

Out!

Not for another two years, you're not

BYERS 'HAD SCREW LOOSE'

by Our Rail Staff **Lynda Lee Potters Bar**

"HOW could it have happened so soon after the previous disasters?" That is what the country is asking as investigators sift through the evidence of yet another disaster involving Stephen Byers.

Says one expert, "It's a clear case of points failure. Mr Byers has failed to grasp *any* of the points about Rail Safety made over the last ten years.

"Byers was an accident waiting to happen," he continued, "and now the inevitable has taken place, Byers has not resigned."

Said a typical commuter, "We have to take Byers every day because there is no alternative. But we have no confidence in him and it is a daily white knuckle ride with him operating the system."

LATE NEWS

● The departure of Mr Byers has been delayed again.

BLAIR CALLS FOR NEW FUNDING SYSTEM

by Our Political Staff **Simon "Hugh" Heffer**

THE SHOCK revelation that the Labour Party accepted a £100,000 donation from a leading figure in the adult entertainment industry (porn), Mr Dirty Desmond, has prompted the government to call for a new method of funding political parties.

Said Mr Blair, "This proves once and for all that politicians like myself cannot be trusted to finance their campaigns with any degree of integrity.

"The temptation is just too much," he continued, "and even when money is offered to me by an obvious sleaze merchant like my friend Des, I cannot resist it."

He concluded, "I feel sure that the taxpayer will want to foot the bill for all political parties on the basis that only then can I be relied upon to act honestly."

Mr Tony Blair is £100,000.

"The lawyers are having a field day"

ASTERIX   OBELIX   XENOPHOBIX

POP STAR NOT GAY SHOCK

by Our Entire Staff

A MAN last night told an astonished nation, "Yes, I am not gay."

He continued, "It's no big deal. My friends and family have known about this for ages. They're perfectly okay about it and I don't see why it should affect my career."

Experts were, however, sceptical about these claims.

"I think the man is being a bit naïve. The vast majority of men in Britain are gay and coming out as a heterosexual could well turn out to be a mistake for him."

However, the man's supporters cite other instances of men confessing to being "straight" without adverse consequences. Said one, "Elton John once said he was straight. And he even got married. And he still sold millions of records."

He continued, "Being a member of a minority group is no disadvantage these days. We salute him for having the courage to admit that he's glad to be not gay."

WHAT YOU MISSED

EXCLUSIVE TO ALL TV CHANNELS

(Horst Wessel Song over shots of Nuremberg Rally)

Presenter, J. Paxman *(for it is he)*: The French have just elected their first Nazi President. But could it happen here? The chilling answer is – it already has. Here is our special report from Britain's racist front-line, Neasden-under-Lyme.

(Shot of solitary pimply youth in anorak standing in shopping precinct trying to hand out BNP leaflets to bored shoppers)

Voice-over: In last May's council elections, the BNP won a frightening 0.8 percent of the vote here in Neasden-under-Lyme.

This means, following the rise to power of far-right groups all over Europe, it could be as high as 105 percent. And that's excluding such factors as September 11, the Middle East crisis, the collapse of ITV Digital and the searing new question mark over the availability of David Beckham for the World Cup. That is why the voters are now in their millions signing up to the gospel of hatred peddled by the extreme right.

Surely it is only a matter of time before the cobbled streets of this sleepy Midlands seaside town echo to the grim tramp of jack-boots. This is George Origami returning you to the studio.

(Cut to presenter with three men in suits)

Paxperson: I am joined by three men in suits representing all shades of mainstream political opinion. Gentlemen, democracy is under threat as it has not been since the dark days of 1940. How should we react? Should the allies invade France and restore democracy by force, if necessary putting Osama Le Pen on trial for war crimes?

First Man In Suit: I think we're all agreed on that.

Paxperson: I'm sorry, I'll have to interrupt you there because we've run out of time. Goodnight, and let's hope that you don't get a knock on the door from the Fascists in the middle of it!

(Credits Roll)

Un Taxi Driver Ecrit

Chaque semaine, un well-known chauffeur de taxi écrit sur un important issue de nos jours.

CETTE SEMAINE:
"L'Election Français" par **Jean-Marie le Cabbie** (numéro 732487).

Sacre bleu, gouveneur! Cet Le Pen, eh? Tout le monde are knocking him, mais il a un point, n'est-ce pas? Je veux dire, les asylum seekers, par example, sponging off notre economie! La guillotine est trop bonne pour eux!! C'est la seule langue ils comprendent!

J'ai eu cette Barbara Amiel dans la derrière de mon taxi une fois! Quelle scorcheur n'est-ce pas? Et un very clever woman.

SEMAINE PROCHAINE: Simone Heffeur (no. 63742) on "Pourquoi Enoch avait raison".

BLUNKETT SHOCK

Schools are being swamped by children who know nothing about this country and can hardly speak English...

...and then there are the asylum seekers' children as well

THE BYERS TAPESTRY

ME AND MY SPOON

THIS WEEK

NO. 94
SIR IAN McKELLEN

Would you describe yourself as a spoon-lover?

Of course. It isn't only straight people who like spoons, you know. That's the mistake you lot in the media are always making. Gay people can love spoons quite as much as anyone else.

If I may just change the subject, are there any particular types of spoon which you prefer?

Look, I just said that I like the same sort of spoons as anyone else. What are you expecting me to say, that I only like 'pink spoons', or 'bent spoons'? You people are all the same, trying to force us back into the ghetto.

Can I change the subject again? In your childhood, was yours a happy home with plenty of spoons in it?

There you go again. It's the old unhappy childhood, spoon deprivation equals homosexual theory. It's nonsense. There were as many spoons in our household as any other.

Sir Ian, can I come to your new film, which is why you've agreed to do this interview? Do spoons feature at all in the film?

Yes, I play the wizard Gandalf, an intensely taxing role which makes huge demands on the actor. I am really the character around whom the whole story revolves. It's a mythic journey about cosmic redemption…

But are there any spoons, Sir Ian?

Really, to drag in something as trivial as spoons betrays an unconscious but entirely typical homophobia which is almost endemic in British society, from Tony Blair downwards.

Has anything amusing ever happened to you in connection with a spoon?

Oddly enough, Noel Coward had a very funny story about Terry Rattigan and a soup spoon…

You're meant to say 'no'.

NEXT WEEK: Lord Haskins – "Me and My Mousemat".

END OF AN ERA AS NATION MOURNS

by Our Royal Staff Lady Antonia Holden

TRIBUTES poured in from all over the country following the announcement that Britain's best-loved granny Esther Rantzen had passed away from the BBC at the age of 102.

"We shall never see her like again," said a black-tied and visibly moved Peter Sissons, as he read out the newson News 24. "She exemplified all that was best about Britain – she combined an unfailing dedication to public service with a wicked sense of fun, which helped to hold the nation together doing the dark days of the 1920s."

That's Death

Queen Esther was the patroness of hundreds of charities and became Britain's most famous widow following the tragic death of her husband King Desmond.

For decades she kept the nation enthralled with her radiant toothy smile, her faithful entourage of camp young men in fluffy jumpers and her collection of strangely-shaped vegetables.

Yesterday, in silent tribute, members of the public were laying phallic-shaped carrots outside the BBC, as they queued to sign the Book of Relief that she would never be seen on television again.

Perhaps the most moving tribute was that which came from the famous "Talking Dog", who appeared many times with Queen Esther saying the word "sausages". Last night he summed up the mood of the nation when he told reporters "sausages".

COURT CIRCULAR

BECKINGHAM PALACE
Their Royal Highnesses the Posh and Poshess of Becks graciously received a number of guests at a special reception to mark the commencement of the World Cup. The procession was as follows:

First Stretch Limousine
Sir David Frostie and Lady Ocarina of Weston Supertoseeyou

First Helicopter
Mr Mohamed Al-Fugger of Harrods with his bodyguard Ex-Chief Inspector Backhander of the Metropolitan Police Force

Second Stretch Limousine
Her Royal Highness the Joan of Collins with her husband Darby; ex-TV's the Cilla of Black and her Lady-in-Waiting Mrs Dale Winton; Sir Angus of That Deayton; Sir Richard Beardie of Virgin; Sir Elton of Candlewind and partner; TV's Mr Graham Norty

Third Stretch Limousine
Mr Jamie Allover, Mrs Jules Allover and their baby Ms Sainsbury Allover

First Team Coach
His Excellency Sven-Bonkin Ericsson and his fiancée Principessa D'Ollio Di Yum Yum; various other men in ill-fitting suits believed to be Prince Edward of Sherringham, Lord David of Seaman and Sir Nickswell Butt *(Who he? Ed.)*

Man In Dirty Mac
Richard "Dirty Desmond", Pornographer-in-Chief to His Highness Tony Blair

The Day I Met The Queen

by **Johnny Freedland** (Age 7)

ONE day I was invited to go to Windsor Castle and meet the Queen! Gosh, fancy me, the world's leading Republican and top Guardian thinker, meeting a real live Monarch! Phew!

Windsor Castle is jolly big and there were lots of people there but even so the Queen stopped and spoke to me. She was very nice but was not wearing a crown like she does on the banknotes.

"Hello," she said, smiling, but I was determined to stick to my principles as the world's leading Republican and top Guardian thinker, so I refused to curtsey and call her "Ma'am".

Instead, I fell to my knees and called her "Your Gracious Majesty".

All in all, it was a lovely day and one I shall remember for the rest of my life. God Save The Queen!

© *Rubbisher and Moron Publications.*

THE DAILY TELEGRAPH Friday, May 3, 2002

Iain Duncan Smith Had 'Stripper' Granny

BY DAILY TELEGRAPH POLITICAL STAFF MADDY TUPP

MR DUNCAN SMITH is not at all boring, it was revealed yesterday.

Documents released to the Daily Telegraph show that his paternal grandmother, Eunice Cough, briefly earned a living in the 1920s by modelling corsets for Trimbodice of Leicester.

In 1923, the young Miss Cough (who later married Group Captain "Buffy" Duncan DSO) was featured in a series of advertisements which were never published, due to a strike by compositors at the Leicester Mercury.

A family spokesman told the Telegraph yesterday, "This is the third bogus attempt to make Iain interesting that you have published this week. When will you give up and leave us alone?"

COUGH GETS TOUGH

Duncan Smith: Tory joke

by Our Political Staff **Benny Lin**

IN HIS most dramatic move since becoming the man no one's heard of *(surely "Leader of the Conservative Party"? Ed.)*, Iain Duncan Cough yesterday stamped his authority on the Tory Party by summarily sacking one of his most senior frontbenchers, Ann Witteron, the Shadow Minister of Fish.

No sooner had it been leaked to a Sunday newspaper that Mrs Widderspoon had told the worst joke ever recorded in the history of the world than Duncan Cough sprung into action.

This was the amazing minute-by-minute timetable of terror that rocked the Tory Party to its foundations.

Saturday

11.41pm Mrs Widmerpool is asked to draw the raffle prizes at the Congleton rugby club annual dinner and dance.

11.42 She regales drunken audience with world's worst joke.

11.43 Mr Ted Nargely uses mobile phone to ring through to the Sunday Mirror.

Sunday

9.00 am Sunday Mirror hits newsstands with screaming headline "HUGE RACE ROW ROCKS TORIES: WILL COUGH ACT?"

10.15 Cough strolls down to village shop to purchase Sunday Telegraph and a bumper pack of throat lozenges (honey and menthol).

10.16 While perusing fascinating article by Dr Barkworth on the Single European Fish, Cough's eye strays to Sunday Mirror front page. He is horrified.

10.17 Cough begins frenzied round of calls to all his top advisers. "What do I do?" he asks.

11.20 Cough decides to act. He realises that this is the worst crisis to hit his party since Black Tuesday (the day William Hague wore a baseball cap). Firm intervention, he realises, is the only way to save his party.

12.30 Cough enjoys pre-lunch sherry with Mrs Cough while discussing next move.

1.00 Luncheon is served at Strepsil Manor while the Tory leader ponders the best course of action.

2.30 Cough enjoys Churchill-style power nap in front of quarter-finals of Embassy snooker.

3.00 Cough wakes from nap and springs into action. Asks Mrs Cough to put on kettle.

4.10 Refreshed by cup of Twinings Earl Grey and a handful of throat-soothing cherry-flavoured Zubes, Cough nerves himself to bite the bullet.

4.11 Cough begins to mow lawn.

5.15 Cough remembers he hasn't yet dealt with Mrs Winterbottom. He re-enters house to ring Central Office for further advice.

5.30 He finally gets through to the weekend desk officer at Tory Central Office, who tells him "Don't worry, Mr Cough, it's all been taken care of. We put out a statement saying that you'd sacked her two hours ago."

5.31 Cough celebrates with cup of Lemsip and cracks open new packet of Tunes.

Monday

9.00 am Cough is delighted to read in his Daily Telegraph the headline "Action Man Cough Cracks Down On Tory Fascists".

What You Missed
THAT WINTERTON JOKE IN FULL

"There was a Cuban, a Japanese, an Irishman and a Pakistani, all stuck in a lift. Hang on, no I think I've got that wrong. Maybe it was an Irishman, a Jewish gentleman and a coloured person all sitting in a hot air balloon. Or was it a train? Anyway, one had to be thrown off. So they threw out the Pakistani chap, at least I think it was him, and the Englishman said... oh, I forgot to say that he was there too... he said, 'We've got to chuck out this Paki because there are too many of them coming over here and stealing all our jokes.' I think I've got that right. Or perhaps it was that they are selling balloons for 10 a penny. Anyway, it was very funny when I first heard it. But I'm afraid I'm not very good at telling jokes. I'm better at talking about fish, which is my job. Or at least it was until I told this joke."

(Taken from the Conservative Central Office Book of After-Dinner Jokes, with foreword by Lord Archer)

SPOT THE TALIBAN

LOOK closely at this photograph. Can you see any members of the Taliban? Or Al Qaeda? Or indeed anyone else?

If you can, mark the spot with an X, and send to:

Mr Geoff Hoon, Ministry of Defence, London SW1.

He will then send a detachment of 1000 highly-trained Royal Marines to blow up everything in sight, at a cost of only £20 million.

Dr Stutterfraud writes

THE LATEST video pictures of Osama bin Laden show a marked deterioration in his health. In particular, his right hand exhibits all the symptoms of a degenerative disease that is turning him into the devil – *manus shrivelensis satanicus*, to give it the full medical name. What happens is that the fingers grow more and more evil until they become flesh-ripping talons which can be used to dissect his victims before they are eaten alive. The only remedy is to bomb Iraq. *(Can this be right? Ed.)*

© Dr Utterfraud, Timestrash

THE WASHING
...TIONS CAREFULLY
...DONT MAKE A
...UP OF MY BEST
...BIT OF KIT

MACHINE	HAND WASH
WARM MIN WASH (40°C)	WARM (40°C)

...structions, lycra cycling shorts

that it is someone intending to case people's homes with a view to burgling them.
"A uniformed Fire Service employee, with identification, can provide this service free of charge upon request."

Manchester Metro News

"We are all ears to your requirements or needs and are committed to ensuring your total satisfaction. In the unlikely event of this happening, please let us know"
Chateaux de Charme

...n Secretary, Jack Frost, has said: "Where we allow ...es to disintegrate or states to fail, we put at risk the basis ...bal society itself."
Sydney Morning Herald

Margaret Thatcher, a unique figure in global politics, shares her views about the opportunities and dangers of the new millennium.

(161) **EXCL. EDITION**
OFFER price 1p
PAPERBACK

World Books

hyhyhyhyyhy
hyhyhyyhy

SDLP Mayor of Coleraine John Dallat has called on the RUC to revoke prisoner early release licences after a spate of pipe bomb attacks in Derry

Irish Times

Det Sgt Doug Marshall, said inquiries will be carried out in the area.
He said: "Obviously it makes it that much more difficult for the police when crimes are reported after the event."

Evening Mail

16.03 Train Delayed
15:55 Southend Central to London Fenchurch Street due 17:15
This train has been delayed at Southend Central and is now 6 min late.
This is due to Police putting yobs on train.

C2C Rail Website

...ersity of Zimbabwe letterhead

The FRIENDLY INN
Tel: 01422 365287
Hovenden Road, Hovenden, Halifax
Thurs 2nd Aug Live Show
WAR NIGHT All Welcome

Local Newspaper

Boris Johnson discusses Uganda
Daily Telegraph

In spite of fears that the defeat of the Taliban government might reduce numbers, this turned out to be considerably larger than the October 13th march and rally with at least 50,000 taking part. This time the demonstration was organised by the "Stop the Wart Coalition"

Non-Violent Resistance Network newsletter

8.30 The Most Evil Men And Women In History
Quentin Willson reveals some of the more fanciful excuses given by speeding motorists to avoid picking up points on their licences, while Tiff Needell test-drives the new MGTF.

Hot Tickets, Evening Standard

Nick Griffin: Accused of illegal fund-raising

Independent

Spoons Big and Small

...m a phenomenal paddle spoon by Bill ...hipps to Julie Arkell's paper creations, ...e gallery presents an innovative mixed media spoon exhibition.

Lesley Craze Gallery

Lord Callaghan, the former Labour leader, was one of the first to arrive with his daughter, Baroness Jay, Tony Blair's former leader in the House of Lords. Lord Callaghan was resplendent in a black sequinned dinner suit and pearl choker.

Daily Telegraph

9.00 FILM Disturbing Behaviour (David Nutter, 1998) (T) (S) Mediocre thriller
Observer

...Mr Duncan suggested his sex- ...ality had held him back from ...omotion, and said: "If I were ...arried with two kids I might ...e in a different position."

Evening Standard

● Official world wankings: 1 Tiger Woods (USA) 16.53, 2 Phil Mickelson (USA) 10.85, 3 Ernie Els (RSA) 7.27, 4 Retief Goosen (RSA) 7.06,

Dundee Courier

Police are using a severed finger found at the scene of a bungled break-in to track a burglar... They are using DNA from the digit to track the thief, who left empty-handed.

Ceefax, 23/7/02

Lords: Debates on weapons of mass destruction in Iraq and public services;

The Daily Telegraph

23 Nights Departing October 14th
NO FLYING! Dover, Gibraltar, Sardinia, Malta, Sicily, Itea (Greece), Transit Corinth Canal, Piraeus (overnightt), Santorini, Rhodes, Crete, Lampedusa (Pelagie Islands), Tunisia, Motreil (Spain), Dover.
CRUISE WORLD'S BULK PURCHASE OF CABINS! GUARANTEED OFFER!
NO FLYING!

Cruise World advertisement

Shool's positive ethos praised
Wilts Standard

Head of Chef
Required 12K p.a.
Chinese Take-Away in Kent
Advertisement, Kent & Sussex Courier

'Vivacious' was the word most often used, and there were repeated mentions of the fact that she actually had a fine brain, even though she had not been allowed to go to university, these being the days when clever young aristocratic women were considered intellectual if they finished a course in cat-maintenance.

Observer (on Princess Margaret)

The reconstituted interdepartmental working group on transsexuals would do well to make sure it uses the transsexual community's expertise in ensuring that the sort of half-cocked legal mess that exists in the US is not created here.

The Times

THE BOOK OF SHARON

Chapter 94

1. And lo, it came to pass at the Feast of the Passover that an Hamas-ite came privily unto the tents of the children of Israel, while they sat at meat, and did slay them all, even unto himself.

2. And among the children of Israel there were slain both man and woman, old and young alike.

3. And when he heard it, Sharon waxed terrible in his wrath, and rent his garments, saying "Woe unto the Araf-ites and the Hamas-ites and the Hez-bollites."

4. "Verily, I say, this time they have goneth too far."

5. Then Shar-on rose up and summoned his hosts and his chariots of fire, and sayeth unto them "Go forth, even unto the city of Jen-in and lay it waste."

6. "For I tell you that only when one stone shall not remain upon another shall peace be brought to the land of Israel."

7. Then went they forth at his bidding, and did as he had commanded, crying out, "All these things we do we are doing in the name of peace."

8. And first they visited upon the city of Jen-in a terrible plague of fire and brimstone, so that many of the Araf-ites and Hamas-ites were slain, even men, women and children. And among the Arab-ites there was much wailing and gnashing of teeth.

9. And it was as Shar-on had commanded, so that by nightfall the city of Jen-in was laid waste, so that not one stone remained upon another.

10. And those that stood by and gazed upon that place likened it unto a desert beset by a plague of locusts where not even the cockatrice hath a place to lay its young in the dust.

11. Or like unto the sands of Eilat when the makers of holiday have departed and have decided to go somewhere safer this year even unto the place called Tur-key or possibly Du-bai.

12. Then Sharon rejoiced and said unto the children of Israel, "See how I have slain all our enemies, the Hamas-ites and the Araf-ites and the Hezboll-ites, and all those who seek to destroy us and our children and our children's children."

13. "Thus have I done as I promised you, and brought peace at last to the land of Israel."

14. And, indeed, it came to pass that for a short while there was silence in the land, and it looketh to Shar-on that this had doneth the trick.

15. But, lo, even as ye have guessed, it came to pass that another Hamas-ite came privily to the tents of the children of Israel, to slay them in the place that is called Snoo-ker.

16. And thus it was, even as the prophet had foretold, that it was back to the square that is called one. *(To be continued for ever)*

THOMAS *THE PRIVATISED TANK ENGINE*
Part 94: Thomas and the Big Fib
BY THE REV. TAWDRY

THOMAS was feeling very sad, after Gordon had gone off the rails at Potters Bar.

"I hope it won't happen to me," he told the Fat Controller, Mr Jarvis.

"Don't worry, Thomas," said the Fat Controller, going red. "It was just a case of sabotage. Not our fault at all. I mean, that's why it's not going to happen again."

"But surely," broke in Henry from the next siding, "everyone is agreed that your man forgot to put the screws back in the points?"

"I think it's time you went on a long journey, Henry," said the Fat Controller, getting very angry.

And that's why next morning Henry was sold off to Malaysian Railways, and Mr Jarvis lived happily ever after.

'I forgive Tony' says his tearful partner Cherie

by Our Current Affairs Staff **Steven Gloverat**

A TEARFUL Cherie Booth told reporters today that she was prepared to stand by her wayward partner Tony, following revelations that he had "a sordid relationship" with a known vice king.

Said Cherie: "I had no idea Tony was up to this sort of thing behind my back. It is a sort of schizophrenia. One minute he is the Prime Minister meeting heads of state, the next he is taking rolled-up twenty-pound notes from a sleazy porn merchant."

Angus Deayton

But last night a tearful Tony admitted his mistake. "I have upset my loved ones and let a lot of people down. But it is time to draw a line under the whole business and get on with the rest of my life – namely, taking money from Lord Sainsbury instead."

"We found these under your mattress and we're worried you're getting into politics!"

Rigorous New Tests for St Cake's Entry

End to 'Putting Down At Birth'

By Our Education Staff **Cilla Blackboard and Lynda Chalk**

IN THE biggest revolution in its 450-year history, St Cake's, the exclusive West Midlands School, is to introduce new "entrance tests" to ensure that all would-be pupils have an equal chance of gaining entry to the school.

Said headmaster Mr Kipling, "It will no longer be possible for Old Cakeians to put their sons down at birth and be assured of a place."

Frightfully Common Entrance

Under the new system, all prospective entrants to the school will have to sit a series of special new IQ-based tests.

Sample questions might include the following:

St Cake's Entrance.
Time allowed: 5 minutes.

Verbal Reasoning

1. Fill in the words missing from the following sentence.
My parents are . . .

   A. Quite well off ☐

   B. Very very rich ☐

   C. Living abroad for tax purposes ☐

2. If the fees at a well-known boarding school are £20,000 a term, will your father . . .

   A. Pay but complain under his breath as he does so? ☐

   B. Pay and not notice? ☐

   C. Pay a bit extra to ensure that you get in? ☐

3. That's it.

MAN KICKS BALL

THE ENTIRE world held its breath last night as a man kicked a ball.

Amazed onlookers were left open-mouthed when the ball that the man kicked went into a net. "We haven't seen anything like this", said one expert, "since this morning."

On other pages

■ That Man – In-Depth Profile **2,3,4,5**

■ That Kick – Amazing Pix **6,7,8,9**

■ How The Man Kicking the Ball Touches All Our Lives – Editorial **10**

■ What Happens When a Man Kicks a Ball, Dr Stuttaford writes **11**

■ Nuclear War Breaks Out on Subcontinent **94**

World Cup 2002 Official Sticker Collection

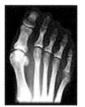
Beckham

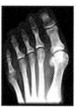
Gerrard

Neville

Dyer

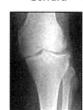
Butt

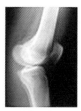
Murphy

ENGLAND

SALLY JOCKSTRAP
At the World Cup

Tokyo, Tuesday
Make no mistake, England United are going all the way! Pakistan never stood a chance as High Chapparal romped home at 40-1 to square the series.

Seoul, Friday
What a turn up for the books! Michael Schumacher was a lonely figure as he trudged back to the pavillion after the umpire gave him a red card on the 18th hole. No wonder Mike Tyson is looking forward to the rematch.

Wembley, Saturday
What's happened to the England team? I know they've had problems with injuries, but you would think that at least one player could pull on a red shirt and turn out for the national side at this most famous of all stadiums. *(You're fired. Ed)*

Six To Watch

Your guide to the key players who will make World Cup 2002 the greatest sporting event in the history of the universe.

Evostik
Serbia's No. 3 shirt, this giant defender has been sent off 27 times and is currently on trial for war crimes at the Hague. He hopes to be available if Serbia come top of the Group of Death including Bosnia, Croatia and the little-fancied Macedonia.

M'Bargo Machete
Rumbabwe's dangerous "General of the Midfield", Machete is a veteran of numerous campaigns (none of them to do with football) and is justly feared throughout Africa.

Kik Ohn Gol
North Korea's No. 5 shirt, the man they call the maestro of the back four. He is his nation's top goal-scorer with 498 own goals to his name. He is expected to be executed after the Quarter Finals.

Bishop Asil Nadir
From the Anglo-Catholic wing of the Church, Bishop Nadir is a fluent Chinese speaker and is a strong supporter of the castration of women priests. *(Surely "safe pair of hands"? Can you check this one out? Ed.)*

El Snorto
Full name Carlo y Jesus Calobar Diablo Romera di Goya *(That's enough full name. Ed.)*, Colombia's keeper is looked to as the saviour of his nation's failing squad. A renowned distributor in his country, El Snorto is hoping to make a lot of money selling cocaine to other players during the finals.

Gaza
Palestine's explosive No. 7 shirt (the famous Gaza Strip), Gaza Hamas is the only player left from the original squad sent to wipe out the Israeli team on their way to destroying the World Cup. *(That's enough Six To Watch. Ed.)*

"Oh no! Boris dancers"

POLLY FILLER

ON THE WORLD CUP

OH no! It's the event I've been dreading for the last four years, when the useless Simon goes into purdah for weeks, locks himself in a darkened room with the TV and only emerges to refill his beer belly with lager.

Yes, it's the World Cup – when men all over the world challenge each other for the Cup of being the most selfish and insensitive creatures on the planet.

And it's not just Simon – the toddler Charlie is beginning to display decidedly useless qualities as well – refusing to change out of his England shirt when he goes to bed and kicking the Nigerian au pair(!) on the grounds that they are going to knock us out of the Group of Death! Really – Men! They're just like toddlers, even the toddlers!

But I'll tell you what really gets on the Filler nerves – the thought of all the work we women will have to do to allow the male of the species (Homo stupidens!) to gorge themselves on the Football Fest – I've been wearing myself out explaining to the au pair how to use the washing machine and photocopying the A-Z so the hopeless girl can do the school run without ending up in Lagos!

LOOK – don't get me wrong! I love football. Beckham's legs! Mmmm! Cuddly little Michael Owen! Bless! And all the other good-looking ones whose names I can't remember! Yummy!! But no one in their right minds (ie, women) would want to watch more than a minute of it.

That's why I'm booking a holiday in Dubai for the duration, where I will shop for shoes and pamper myself with a few expensive beauty treatments.

That'll teach men like Simon to be so selfish!
© *Polly Filler.*

Alternative Rocky Horror Service Book

Service To Be Used During The Staging Of A World Cup Football Match

President: We are not gathered here today, because we've all stayed at home to watch the match on television.

No One: Amen.

(The President shall here run as fast as he can to the Vicarage to ascertain the score)

YES! IT'S WORLD WAR FEVER

by Our Sports Staff **India Nightmare** and **William Kashmir**

ONLY A few days to go now before the big match kicks off, and the Eye's team will be there to bring you up-to-the-minute reports of the bombs as they go off.

The two teams are evenly matched, with India having a slight edge with numerical depth and playing a 4-2-4 megaton formation.

Nuclear Bombay

Pakistan should not be dismissed, possessing an impressive strike force and having been engaged in a long build-up to this final to end all finals.

Group of Total Death

Says Pakistan's manager, General Mustapha War, "We can go all the way to Delhi and wipe them out."

His Indian counterpart, Mr Rajpayload, replied "We are going to take the Pakistanis out. We are going to take no prisoners. They think it's all over – it is going to be now for everybody."

WEST LONDON SQUATTERS DIG IN

'They Can't Kick Us Out' Says Man With Beard

by Our Kensington Palace Correspondent **Grace N. Favour**

A MIDDLE-AGED couple who for years have 'squatted' in one of London's most prestigious housing complexes were last night breathing defiance at suggestions that they should move out.

"Why should people like us be picked on by society," said foreign-born 'traveller' Princess Michael of Kent. "We haven't done anything – why should we leave?"

Right Pair of Kents

"She's right," said her bearded partner, known only to fellow-squatters as 'Prince Michael of Kent'. "We've been living here peaceably for years, not giving trouble to anyone – and yet suddenly the authorities want to chuck us out.

"We've got nowhere to go," he complained bitterly, "except a large house in Gloucestershire.

"They used to call this a free country, in the years when we could stay here for free," said the embittered squatters' spokesman.

Getting The Pushy

The couple are known to supplement their state benefits by hiring themselves out to commercial concerns as look-alikes for the Czar Nicholas II of Russia and Miss Jerry Hall, the model and former partner of Sir Michael Shagger.

"This shaving mirror's not very effective"

ROY of the ROMPERS

IT'S THE BIG MATCH BETWEEN ULRIKA WANDERERS AND NANCY ATHLETICO

GREAT TACKLE SVEN!

I PREFER TO KEEP THAT PRIVATE

IT'S A PLAYING AWAY GAME!

FOR TOP COACH SVEN COR-NICEONESSON IT'S A TOUGH CHALLENGE...

WHAT'S YOUR DEFENCE SVEN?

ER...I'M SWEDISH... IT'S WHAT WE DO...

THEY THINK IT'S ALL OVERSEXED - IT IS NOW!

BUT AS THE WHISTLE IS BLOWN BY THE PRESS, ULRIKA WANDERERS IS THE LOSER

IT WAS OVER FOR US BEFORE IT BEGAN

JUST LIKE THE WORLD CUP

COME ON YOU RED FACES

J COOPER.

X of the CENSOREDS

I'M GAGGING FOR IT!

...I'M GAGGING EVERYONE!

DID YOU SCORE, X?

THAT'S SUB JUDICE!

THEY THINK IT'S LEG OVER...

...BUT THEY'RE NOT ALLOWED TO SAY!

WRITS OUT FOR THE LADS!

J COOPER.

ROY of the SKID ROVERS

MELCHESTER UNITED ARE IN DESPERATE FINANCIAL STRAITS AFTER THE COLLAPSE OF ITV DIGITAL...

♪ WHO'S THE BASTARD IN BLACK?

♪ COME ON YOU IN THE REDS ♪

I'M THE OFFICIAL RECEIVER

OH DEAR

P 45

HE'S BRINGING ROY OFF!

GO!!!!!

J COOPER.

YOU WERE ALWAYS GOOD IN THE BOX ROY

I'VE BECOME INVISIBLE JUST LIKE ITV DIGITAL

FOOTBALL'S BECOMING HOMELESS ♪

ENGLAND FANS SHAME THE NATION

by **E.I. Addio**, Our Man In The Sushi Bar With A Bowl Of Rice And A Glass Of Water

HUNDREDS of new-look English fans rampaged through the streets of Seoul yesterday, chanting "Hats off to Brazil, they were the better team on the day."

The fans were reported to be "sober out of their minds" and went out of their way not to break any windows or urinate in anyone's doorway.

Said one shocked Korean, "We are amazed that this sort of behaviour goes on. We had been looking forward to spraying them with CS gas and locking them up in our prisons for hundreds of years."

Said a spokesman for the English fans, "We are unrepentant. All the other teams in this tournament are truly terrific. We have really enjoyed the football and feel much better for not having drunk much for the last month."

A Cab Driver Writes

Every week a taxi driver is asked to comment on an issue of topical importance.

THIS WEEK: **Stan Bummer** (Cab No. 7426385) on England's failure to reach the semi-finals of the World Cup.

...Honestly, guv, there's no way you can blame Seaman, any way you look at it it was a freak goal, I mean, after all, he's kept us in more games than I've driven people to Heathrow via Stansted ha ha ha... but really when you see the replay you've got to question what he was doing off his line, it's a schoolboy error basically, what was he thinking about? Pony-tailed git – and then crying about it – I ask you. I think he should be strung up – on the crossbar? Or maybe shoot himself – except he'd probably miss. It's all his fault we lost. What a bastard!

I 'ad that Gazza in the back of the cab. Threw up all over the seats.

What is your first memory of a spoon?

My father, who was a barrister, was totally blind so I used to have to guide his spoon into the top of his boiled egg. And he used to recite great chunks of Shakespeare to me as I helped him with his soldiers.

In your career at the bar, did you encounter many cases involving spoons?

Oh yes. There was a very famous case in which I defended a man charged with stealing a Georgian silver spoon from Aspreys. The judge was old Mr Justice Malallieu who fell asleep during my summing up. When he woke up, he sentenced my client to death. It was very funny.

In your other career as a novelist and playwright do spoons loom large?

They do indeed. I was on the set of the television series I had written, "Spoon QC" based on my father, when Johnny Gielgud complained that "Spoon" was a silly name for a QC and could we call him "Fork" instead. In the end we compromised and the character was called "Rumpole".

Have you got a favourite spoon?

I certainly do. It belonged to my father and it featured in one of the Rumpole episodes. I use it now to stir my breakfast glass of champagne. Talking of which, I am getting paid for this, aren't I? I think it's best if you talk to my agent. Shall we say £1800?

Has anything amusing ever happened to you involving a spoon?

Isn't Blair ghastly?

NEXT WEEK: Commander Paddick – *"Me and My Duvet"*.

MI5 PINPOINTS AL QAEDA TARGETS

by Our Intelligence Staff **I.Q. Low**

BRITAIN's intelligence services today revealed that after months of painstaking fieldwork and around-the-clock surveillance activities, they have discovered a complete list of possible Al Qaeda targets in the United Kingdom. Here is that MI5 list in full:

1. The Houses of Parliament
2. Buckingham Palace
3. Er...
4. The Twin Towers in New York
5. Er...
6. That's it.

Queen's Birthday Honours

Arise, Sir Mick

Give me some Viagra, Ma'am, and I'll see what I can do

PRE-SCHOOL NURSERY RHYMES

They're changing chords at Buckingham Palace,
Christopher Robin went down with Alice.
Alice is marrying one of the roadies,
"I believe the Queen is surrounded by toadies,"
Says Alice (Cooper).

And what do you do?

Anything I can get my hands on, Ma'am

'QUEEN, THE MUSICAL' 50th Celebration

by Our Showbiz Staff **Phil Seats**

BEN ELTON today led the tributes as 'Queen, the Musical' reached a milestone few critics would have thought possible – fifty performances in the West End.

"This is an unprecedented achievement for a show this dire," said a clearly emotional Mr Elton, speaking after another matinee performance. "Long may the royalty cheques continue to rain down on me."

After Mr Elton's speech there were fireworks aplenty as disgruntled investors confronted him, demanding to know how soon it would be before "Queen, the Musical" was forced to step aside for yet another revival of The Rocky Horror Show.

50 Glorious Years

By Charles Moore
Editor of the Daily Telegraph

I spent the day of the Queen's Golden Jubilee reading the journal written by my great grandfather, Sir Herbert Moore-Gussett, describing how he had marked the Queen's Coronation in 1953 by planting a commemorative oak tree on the village green. Here are his notes for the speech he made on that occasion to a large crowd of respectful villagers.

"Queen, jolly good chap… oak tree symbol of British greatness… Nelson's flagship… beating the foreigners… repeated by Winston in our generation… only language they understand… three cheers for Qu."

What a vivid glimpse this gives of happier times in a bygone age when everyone knew his place and the circulation of the Daily Telegraph was 10 million copies a day.

But we who have lived through these past 50 years can count ourselves fortunate in many respects. Certainly there are many things about the modern age which seem calculated to annoy us, such as when the cashpoint machine obstinately refuses to dispense the much-needed funds for the taxi to Canary Wharf. Or the ghastly names people use nowadays when they are trying to sell you a cup of coffee, such as "tall skinny latte with wings", the sort of cacophonous popular music one is forced to endure while being kept waiting to be connected on the telephone device.

All such infuriating irritations aside, we must nevertheless accept that life in Britain today is very comfortable. As I look about me at my agreeable home in the middle of rural Sussex, I cannot help thinking how much better off everyone is than they were 50 years ago. And I cannot forget that if I had been born 50 years earlier, I might well have fallen on Flanders field and would not have been able to write this article. This alone, I think, indicates just how grateful we should all be that Her Majesty the Queen is still on the throne.

©Mooretrash Productions 2002

THE DAILY TELEGRAPH

I've Seen It All Before

by W.F. Deedes

THE first Golden Jubilee I remember covering was that of Queen Victoria in 1887. She was a small, dumpy figure dressed in black, but this did not *(Continued 1894)*

That Jubilee Lunch Menu in full

Brownnose Windsor Soup

Tongue in Aslic

Groveldlax

– ✳ –

Toadie-In-The-Hole

– ✳ –

Creeps Suzettes

THE JUBILEE YEAR

68

PARTY AT THE PALACE

LENNY HENRY: Wooh! Wooh! Yeahawrigh! Wooh! Teyawor, I'm HUMUNGOUSLY excited to be here on this HUMUNGOUSLY exciting day!!!! Blimey – just think – Buckingham Palace – not yer average council house, is it, eh?!!!!!! Whoops – I'll prob'ly be EXECUTED for saying that!!!!

Enjoying yourself so far, are you!?! Yeah! I've had a great day so far! What about you? Enjoying yourself so far?! Yeah! Nice place they've got here! Whoops!

But have we got a show for you today!! Atomic KITTEN, everybody! Bluuuuuue!! Emma Bunnnnnnton!!! YEAH! And the humoungously HUMUNGOUS Queeeeeen!!!!! But first, please go CRAZEEEE for S CLUB 7!!!!!!!

S CLUB 7:

Doast arpmoo vinn
Tover farnkyfarnky bee!
Doast arpmoo vinn
Tover farnkyfarnky bee!

LENNY HENRY: Yeah? Howsitgointhen? Enjoying yourself so far, are you? Are you? I said, AAAAAARE YOOOOOOOU? I've had a great day so far – and I'm BLACK!!!!!! Now let's pay tribute to those HUMUNGOUSLY HUGE voices that made up the LEGENDARY sound of MOTOWN – Ladies and Gentleman, Emma Bunton IS The Supremes!!!!

EMMA BUNTON:

babylovemybabylove
babylovemybabylove
babylovemybabylove
babylovemybabylove
thank you

BEN ELTON: Emma Bunton, liezungennelmun! Awesome! A truly awesome performance there! What a totally awesome and extraordinarily scarifying performance, liezungennelmun – conveying the truly awesome PAR OF ROCK!!

What about that foobaw, then, eh?? Talk about foobaw!! It's not just BLOKES kickin' a ball about – oh no! BURPY-FART! There – said it! NERDY-GIT-FARTY-PIG! Way-hey – bit CLOSE TO THE EDGE there, eh? EH? Too far – whaddya think?!! Heads-off time for Uncle Ben, eh?! EH?!

Fifty years, liezungennulmun, it's about fifty years of nashnaw unity, fifty

As told to
CRAIG BROWN

years of a truly awesome and noble lady resplendent on her throne, fifty years of CUTTING EDGE HUMOUR, liezungennulmun! FARTY-PANTS! Wooh! WEE-WEE! TOILET! BIGGIES! PUBIC HAIR! Yes indeedy!!! And now, it is my deepest and most honoured privilege to introduce a truly awesome legend of international music – put your hands together for the truly legendary – Dame Shirley Bassey!!!!

SHIRLEY BASSEY:

growlfingAAAAAAAAARRRGH!
growlfingAAAAAAAAARRRGH!
growlfingAAAAAAAAARRRGH!
growlfingAAAAAAAAARRRGH!

BEN ELTON: What a truly magnificent and awesome voice, liezungennulmun, wunnerful party, moment of national unity, wunnerful party, we bow down to Her Maj, whoops, went a bit far there, just calling her Her Maj, not Her Majesty – bit close to the bone! – but truly, what an amazing fifty years of truly awesome and dignified public service, liezungennulmun.

TURDY-BIGGY-BOBS!!! Yes indeedy! Let no-one tell me I've lost my social bite! And talkin' otf social bite – what about those nibbles you get at parties – has the caviare they serve these days gone downhill or what? It's more like DOGGY-DOS!!

Seriously though, it is now my privilege to humbly introduce what must be the most truly awesome music ever written in the history of the universe ever. Liezungennulmun, please kneel down and worship the PAR OF ROCK – the ROCK FORCE that is the MIGHTY QUEEN!

FIRST OLD MAN WITH WEEDY VOICE WHO ISN'T FREDDIE MERCURY:

we will we will rock you
we will we will rock you
we will we will rock you

SECOND OLD MAN WITH WEEDY VOICE WHO ISN'T FREDDIE MERCURY:

galley leo galley leo
i will not let you go let me
go i will not let you go let
me go i will not let you go

RUBY WAX: Um. It's um. Wonderful to. Um. Be here.

KERMIT THE FROG: Yes, it sure is wonderful to be here!

RUBY WAX: Yes. It sure is. I mean, it sure is wonderful – to be here. Really um. Wonderful!

KERMIT THE FROG: Have you said all you want to say, Ruby?

RUBY WAX: I'm American! We're both American! You and I – we're American! And – whaddyaknow! – this is England! Hey – that's funny!!!!!

KERMIT THE FROG: Is that it, Ruby?

RUBY WAX: Um. It's wonderful. To. Be here. Um. And now – um – okay – um – um, yes, I'm American! What am I doing here?! Um. I think we're now ready for, um – excuse me, but are we rea…

TOM JONES:

Sex bum, sex bum
You're my sex bum
Sex bum, sex bum
You're my sex bum

ASIAN MOTHER 1: I am not funny, you stupid cow! Not funny at all!

ASIAN MOTHER 2: But I am less funny than you, you stupid cow! I am tip-top not funny!

ASIAN MOTHER 1: Not true! Tip-top! I am so unfunny, you stupid cow, that I am less funny than the least funny person here tonight!

ASIAN MOTHER 2: Ah, tip-top, but that's as maybe. I am so unfunny that the only reason people laugh at me, you stupid cow, is that they feel sorry for me!

ASIAN MOTHERS 1&2: So let's welcome the fantastic Sir Elton John!

SIR ELTON JOHN:

Ar won lurv, buzz impassible
But ar won lurv, ar won lurv
Ar won lurv, but ar won lurv
Buzz impassible but ar won lurv

LENNY HENRY: Wooh! Yeah! Let's rock! Howsitgointhen? Humungous! Are you havin' a good time? Wooh!

BBC1, Jubilee Tuesday, 12.30 – 6.50 pm

David Dimblebore *(for it is he)*: And still they come, the little floats that made Britain everything it is today. And coming down the Mall now are the Royal Women's Volunteer Corps of Dog Handlers. You can see the years of training that have gone into the handling of these dogs, many of them with four legs and tails held proudly aloft in honour of Her Majesty's 50 years on the throne.

And behind them, the Brigade of Queen's Own Lollipop Ladies, looking resplendent in their magnificent Dayglo uniforms, lollipops held proudly aloft. The lollipop lady was, of course, first introduced into Britain in 1969 by Barbara Castle.

(Historian in background: "I think you'll find it was Queen Victoria who was as we all know a great lover of lollipops…")

David Dimblebore… and still they come, and now a wonderful tableau representing life in Britain in the 1970s. There you see the flares, the kipper ties, the long flowing hair, the penny-farthing bicycles. And there's a young couple lying in bed smoking cannabis and watching The Sweeney on one of the tiny little black and white TV sets we had in those days…

(Historian: I think you'll find, David, that that was The Man From U.N.C.L.E., not The Sweeney.)

David Dimblebore: Well, the Duke of Edinburgh's certainly enjoying that, from the way he's sitting there with his eyes closed. I wonder what the Queen thinks?

Ah, and now representing the West End of the 1960s, the cast of the musical Twang!! Isn't that Barbara Windsor there…

(Historian: No, I think you'll find that's Princess Anne, or is it Alan Bennett?)

David Dimblebore: And now, what a wonderfully imaginative touch, the

children of the Ronald Kray Primary School in Wood Green will release special Jubilee balloons in the shape of animals that they've been making under the supervision of their art mistress, Miss R. Sewell. Up they fly, there they go, red, blue, white, all the colours you could think of. A wonderful sight. I think that's a rabbit we can see, if the camera can get close enough, and there's a sausage dog, and there's another and another. Or perhaps in honour of the Queen they could be her favourite corgis?

And now the moment we've all been waiting for – the celebrity float carrying cardboard cut-outs of some of the best-loved celebrities who have entertained us all through the last 50 years. There's, er, Alan Titchmarsh, and isn't that Angela Rippon, and, er, that's Michael Fish, and Peter Snow with his legendary swingometer, swinging away in the sunshine. What wonderful memories they bring back!

And next we have a troupe of those colourful figures of modern London, familiar to all tourists, the sellers of the Big Issue. Many of them have given up their homes in other parts of the world to come here to London to serve the community. And there closing in on them are a splendid body of the Metropolitan Police, the much-loved London 'bobbies', as they present their truncheons and bring them down on the heads of those unfortunate visitors to our shores. I'm sure the young princes are enjoying that spectacle! And so is the Queen, by the way she is looking at her watch!

But now another high point, the massed fly-past of the entire Royal Air Force – no fewer than three aircraft, two of them dating back to the Second World War, as they scream in low overhead, at nearly 100 miles an hour…

(Dimblore continues in similar vein for several hours…)

ULSTER JOINS IN JUBILEE CELEBRATIONS

by Our Northern Ireland Correspondent **Belfast Mooney**

THE JUBILEE celebrations certainly went with a bang in Ulster last night with spectacular fireworks in many of Belfast's streets. All day there were traditional marches, with many of the volunteer groups rep- resented, including the UVF and the IRA.

They were later joined by a large group of uniformed personnel representing the police force and then eventually a number of regiments of the armed forces joined in to provide a climax to a perfect *(cont. p. 94)*

(cont. p. 94)

Lord Desmond of Filth, for services to the Asian community

Sir Keith Vaz, for services to the sleaze industry

Sir Ronald Biggs, for services to crime

Dame Myra Hindley, for services to the newspaper industry

JUBILEE HONOURS LIST IN FULL

OBEs cont'd. from p. 94
for services to waste disposal in the West Midlands; Michael Horovitz, for services to the photocopying industry in Soho; MCPC Jobsworth, for services to the private finance initiative, Redditch; Ken Beard, for services to the Milton Keynes Jazz Festival; Defra Binduja, Ministry of Culture, Media and Sport, for services to Asian netball; Mrs Siobhan Wong, for services to Irish-Chinese charities.

VOLE (Victorian Order of Loyalty to the Empire)
Crispin Gaytrouser, former Comptroller of the Backstairs to Her Majesty the Queen Mother; Horace Campfellow, Keeper of Her Majesty the Queen Mother's Jigsaws; Hon. Teddy Lushington-Lush, Custodian-in-Chief of the Drinks Cabinet to HRH the Princess Margaret; JPS Benson-Rothman, purveyor of tobacco requisites to Her Late Royal Highness; Mrs Camilla Parker-Knowles, Mistress of the Royal Bedchamber, for services to HRH the Prince of Wales.

Overseas Honours
Falkland Islands
OBE Reg Sheepshagger, Penguin Warden at the Goose Green Nature Reserve; Mrs Peggy Kelp, proprietor of the Sir Max Hastings Memorial Tea Rooms, Port Stanley.

Gibraltar
MBE Winston di Gomez, manager of Apes R Us Postcard Shop; Alfonso Massingberd, features editor of *What's On In Gibraltar*.

Ascension Island
PDV Crash, for services to air traffic control.

"More HRT, Vicar?"

Daily Mail

FRIDAY, JUNE 28, 2002

PENSIONS WORTHLESS AS STOCK MARKET COLLAPSE HERALDS HOUSE PRICE DISASTER

'Time to end it all now'

MIDDLE-CLASS newspaper readers might as well top themselves at once, according to a series of reports published every day in the Daily Mail.

by Daily Mail Staff
Clare Monger

The only reason to stay alive, according to experts, is to see whether the Mail runs an even more depressing report the next day, suggesting that it is only a matter of time before economic ruin strikes every man, woman and child in Britain, reducing them to eating their pets and begging for loose change from asylum seekers who (cont. p 94)

COMMENT

How Evil Blair has Tarnished the Queen Mother's funeral

IT should have been a golden memory as we looked back on an occasion which united the nation in grief and pride. Instead, the funeral has become tainted by endless headlines and stories about Downing Street's memos and emails to Black Rod. How could we have let a glorious celebration of British patriotism descend into dreary and trivial political mud slinging? Whoever is responsible should be ashamed of themselves – and that means **you**, Mr Editor. *(Surely "Mr Blair"? Ed.)*

On Other Pages
How Blair tried to muscle his way onto the front page by being Prime Minister.

Why Sir Paul Should Do The Decent Thing And Divorce Heather At Once
Writes GLENDA LEE-POTTY

IT IS only too obvious that Sir Paul McCartney, the world's best-loved composer, has fallen for the oldest trick in the book.

He has become the victim of a ruthless gold-digger who is out to kill him.

It is always the same, when a much-loved and saintly wife and mother tragically passes on, leaving her husband defenceless against the ruthless wiles of a self-appointed wife No. 2 .

Drivel

That is why Paul's children did everything they could to prevent their dear father walking up the aisle to a certain death.

But who is to know that they themselves are now safe?

After Paul swallows his fatal dose of rat poison, how long will it be before the same fate befalls his innocent kiddies?

But it is not too late. It is time for Macca to act now to save himself and his loved ones from this Lucretia Borgia of our times.

Garbage

He must phone the police immediately and tell them all he knows about the plot to bump off the entire McCartney dynasty, so that the murderess can lay her evil hands on one of the world's greatest fortunes.

It will be hard for him to turn in the wife to whom he has been married for only a few days, knowing that she will face death on the gallows.

But he must act now to save himself, his family and civilisation.

© Lynda Lee-Poison, Dacretash Productions 2002

Where Were You When You Heard The News That Black Rod's Killer Memo Had Meant That Downing Street Had To Withdraw Its Complaint To The PCC?

Boris Johnson of the Daily Telegraph

"I was writing an article for the Daily Telegraph, explaining how brilliant the Spectator had been to print Obore's amazing scoop."

Peter Obore of the Spectator

"I was on TV at the time, explaining to Jon Snow how brilliant I had been to break the world's greatest ever scoop."

Black Rod, General Sir Michael Willcockitupforblair

"I was just putting on my black tights in the Lords gents, thinking maybe I'd overdone it a bit by telling that johnny from the Spectator what a ghastly little shit Blair is."

Paul Dacre of the Daily Mail

"I was in my office reading the Spectator when I saw this piece by Peter Obore. I brilliantly decided that no one reads the Spec, so I could run it on the front page of the Mail and everyone would think how brilliant we were."

The Queen

"I was just working out the arrangements for Mr Blair's funeral, and wondering where to put Mr Brown when..."

"Brother Nathaniel, burning a witch is a serious business"

"Do you ever worry that in our rush to get schools online we've neglected core skills?"

COUGH ON CRIME, COUGH ON THE CAUSES OF CRIME

*by Our Political Staff **Peter O'Bore***

IN A dazzling initiative which has left the political world gasping, the leader of the Conservative Party Mr Iain Duncan Cough has decided to remain silent on the dramatic rise in crime figures since the Blair government took power.

This astute move follows Mr Cough's equally dramatic decision to say nothing at all about the sensational Black Rod affair which has rocked the government to its foundations.

As reporters yesterday besieged Mr Cough's country house, Strepsil Manor, begging him to say something about anything at all, the wily Tory leader issued a non-statement to say that he had nothing to say.

Floreat Covonia

Political insiders were last night unanimous in their admiration for Mr Cough's bold Silence Initiative, which has left the Labour Party stunned.

Said one senior Tory, "Iain Cough is growing in stature by the day, with every speech he fails to make."

● Those Cough Silences In Full **p. 0**

FAYED TO CLOSE

By Our Media Correspondent
Mr Punch

LONG-running humorous businessman Mohamed al Fayed finally admitted defeat last night, bringing to an end a comic institution that has kept the nation laughing since the 1980s.

In its heyday, Fayed produced classic jokes such as Tenniel's "Dropping the Piles of Money", Pont's "The British Passport" and H.M. Bateman's "The Man Who Liked Fayed". It was also responsible for long-running features such as "Let's Fuggin' Parler Fuggin' Fugglais".

Curate's Bad Egg

However in recent years Fayed has become lacklustre and has lost most of its audience.

"Fayed just isn't as funny as it used to be," said one media commentator. "Often I would look at Fayed in the dentist's waiting room and barely raise a smile.

"It's probably time to call it a day. Punch is much better off without him."

NURSERY TIMES

(incorporating the Evening Standard)   Friday, July 12, 2002

'I WAS PUSHED' claims Humpty

by Veronica Waddleduck

IN A sensational development that has threatened to ruin the career of the Lord Mayor of Toytown, a Mr Humpty Dumpty, 26, has claimed that he did not fall off the wall, as originally reported, but was pushed by the Lord Mayor.

The rotund former egg told the *Nursery Times* that a scuffle had broken out at a tea party involving the Lord Mayor, Sir Redfaced Ken, and his pregnant live-in partner Little Red Riding Ken.

Rotten Egg

Said Humpty: "The Mayor had consumed a large number of winegums and was acting in a strange manner.

"I was sitting innocently on the wall minding my own business," he continued, "when I heard the Lord Mayor screaming at his partner to stop eating her chocolate cigarette as it would make her sick.

"The next thing I knew, I was lying in pieces on the floor, and all the King's Paramedics were trying to put me together again. But the Lord Mayor had run off into the woods."

Ten questions the Mayor of Toytown must answer

1. How high is the wall that Humpty fell off?

2. Were you the worse for winegums?

3. Is anyone still reading this?

4. Er...

5. That's it.

Mr Dumpty is an employee of the *Nursery Times*

ON OTHER PAGES ● *Incredibly old woman refuses to leave shoe 3* ● *Three little pigs – new foot and mouth scare 4* ● *Gingerbread house on market for £750,000* **94**

RED-FACED KEN

I was as pissed as one of my newts

That Elton John Citation In Full

SALUTAMUS ELTONIUS JOHANNENSIS CANTORUS POPULARIS COMPOSITOR "CANDELLUS IN VENTO" CELEBRATISSIMA CANTATA IN FUNERALIS DIANAE "PRINCIPESSA CORDIUM" ET FAMOSISSIMUS PIANISTUS CUM BIFOCALES LUDICROSSIMI CUM WIGGI GROTESQUI SIMULARITER LIBERACE QUONDAM DENIGRATUS ET VILIFICATUS IN "SOLE" (PAPERIUS MURDOCHENSIS) "POOFTUS NARCOTICUS" VOCATUS SED RECOMPENSATUS AB AWARDUS DAMAGENSIS PUNITIVUS MMMMMM LIBRI (AUT MCCCLXIV EUROS) ATQUE AMATOR FLORIBUNDIUM LILIAE ROSARUMQUE ET NARCISSI ET ULTIME HONORATUS AB BLAIRUS MAXIMUS IMPERATOR "SIR ELTONIUS" ELEVATUS AD EQUES BRITANNICUS CUM "SIR CLIFFUS", "SIR MICKUS", "SIR MACCUS" ET MULTOS ALTEROS PISSPOORICES MUSICIANENSES POPULARES. SALUTAMUS REGINA TANTRUM ET TIARA.

© ACADEMIA REGALIS MUSICUM MMII
(MOTTO: DUMBUS DOWNUS)

WEMBLEY UNIVERSITY HALLS OF RESIDENCE

BOTTLE BANK

VOMIT TANK

WIMBLEDON 2002

SIX TO DROOL OVER

(Surely watch? Ed.)

Krikey Pornakova, 28-year-old super-lovely from the land of Sexlovakia.

Titzi Longlegova, 22-year-old lovely from the land of Rumpymania.

Nika Elastica, 16-year-old Lolita from the land of Pornographia. *(That's quite enough. Ed)*

On other pages: Tennis

Daily Look-In-The-Mirror

WET WIMP LOSES YET AGAIN

by **TIM HENMAN**

HOW PATHETIC! Yet another summer goes by and we have to witness another dismal display by the so-called great hope of British journalism, Piers Morman.

There is only one word to describe his shockingly bad performance against the world's number one tabloid editor, Lleyton Yelland. And that's "loser".

Beforehand, it was all bluster and self-confidence, yet when it came to the great cover price showdown, Moron lost his bottle and choked, giving up without even a whimper. Even the rain showed more guts.

Here's my advice to Panicky Piers: If all you can think of to publish is endless attacks on Tim Henman, then no wonder Yelland walked all over you. You might as well pack it in now. Loser!

On other pages

Those Afghan Lovelies – John Pilger picks his top sexy six **3**
Now It's Snooky – the great new sport **5**
Unfunny cartoon by Rowson **94**

Vot You Missed

That Boris Becker Commentary In Full

Becker: For sure zat one vas out... and if he keeps hitting zem out he vill lose, I am thinking...

Announcer: Game, set and match to Hewitt!

Becker: Now he has lost for sure and ze reason is zat he did not vin as many games as his opponent... zat is vot happens in tennis...
(continued Wimbledon 2003)

Questions Answered

Q: Why do tennis balls have wavy lines on them?

A: The earliest known tennis balls were made in Ancient Egypt, dating from the 3rd Millennium (the reign of King Agassi the 14th). They were made from stones, and featured a wavy hieroglyph showing a stork, a sacred animal associated with the after-life. The first tennis balls in England, referred to in Shakespeare's Henry V, were probably made of sheep's gut stuffed with elderberries. There is unfortunately no record of any markings on these balls, whether wavy or otherwise.

Q: Why do we always speak of "underpants" in the plural? Is there such a thing as a single "pant"?

A: The word "underpants" is derived from the old High German "underpanten", meaning "one who feeds swine with acorns". In the 18th century there was a fashion in Pomerania for a kilt-like garment, worn under the trousers. Because of their "rustic" look, these became known as "Der Trouserpress", from which we get the term in common use today.

Q: Why do people use the exclamation "Great Scott!"? Is there any connection with the famous Polar explorer?

A: No, sadly. This expression is a corruption of the phrase "Grate Scut", meaning the tail of a rabbit (the "scut") used by 18th century parlourmaids to clean out fireplaces or "grates".

Q: Does anyone read that "other bit" of the Times any more, where they now put obituaries and rubbish like this.

A: You are, of course, referring to The Register, which was the original name of The Times, before it became known as The Morning Post. In 1838 *(cont'd. p. 94)*

WOMAN DROPS 'SUICIDE' BOMBSHELL

by Our Political Staff **Barbara Amiel Sharon**

A WOMAN yesterday was severely injured when she walked into a Palestinian charity event crowded with journalists and opened her mouth.

"The whole thing blew up in her face," said a shocked onlooker. "One minute everyone was nodding in agreement with what she was saying and the next there was mayhem as all the hacks ran to phone their newspapers with a scoop.

"You have to feel sympathy with Mrs Blair, though," he continued. "She is hopeless and has no future."

Letters to the Editor

Lady Thatcher's Statue

SIR – I was appalled by the mindless vandalism inflicted on the recently unveiled statue of Queen Boadicea in the Guildhall. Is this the way we treat our heroes now? The assailant would not, of course, have dared confront the Queen in the flesh for fear of her lethal handbag with its iron spikes. What a coward!
Sir Herbert Gussett
The Thatch Cottage, Denis St Pisshead, Dorset.

SIR – If only the statue had been made of rubber then the vandal's iron bar would have sprung back and decapitated him instead, which he thoroughly deserved for his act of gross barbarism against one of the most sublime works of art in history.
Wing Commander R.J.F. Moustache
The Queen's Head, Waldergrave.

SIR – Mrs Thatcher famously went "on and on and on". But now her head has come "off and off and off".
Mike Giggler
Via e-mail.

Letters

The Thatcher Debacle

I was appalled by the mindless attack on the statue of Mrs Thatcher. Why did the man not attack the real person and decapitate her, as she so richly deserves?
Graham Beard
The Student Union, The Royal College of Sparts, Kensington

● Why on earth did this self-styled anarchist choose to attack Mrs Thatcher who is totally irrelevant to modern Britain. The real reactionary Tory Leader is of course, er, none other than Tony Blair who should obviously be assassinated immediately as the true enemy of working people and a running-poodle of US imperialism.
The Rt. Hon. George Michael
The Old Cottage, Goring-on-Thames, Oxon

● Mrs Thatcher famously never lost her head. Until now!
Mike Giggler
Via e-mail

> **Do you have any comments on these letters? Or any comments on the fact that we're always asking for comments? Text us or email us at getalife@sad.co.uk**

Ozymaggias

by Percy Bysshe Sparty

I met a traveller from, er, England
Who said:– A great big lump of stone
Stands in the Guildhall. Near to it, on the carpet,
Half sunk, a shatter'd visage lies, whose frown
And wrinkled lip and sneer of cold command
Tell that its sculptor well those passions read
Which yet survive, stamp'd on these lifeless things,
The hand that mock'd them and the heart that fed.
And on the pedestal these words appear:
"My name is Ozymaggias, queen of queens.
Look on my works, ye mighty, and despair!"

Streets of London 2002

That Diana Fountain Delay Explained

PALACE SUGGESTION

IN MEMORIAM DIANA

GOVERNMENT SUGGESTION

QUEEN OF ♡ RIP

Which would you choose?

Eye Hotline: 088374 267897

'YES – I HAD SOCKS' ADMITS BYERS

by Our Political Staff
Paul Feet

THE FORMER Transport Secretary, Mr Stephen Byers, confessed last night to having socks on when he was involved in a near-naked love-romp with a Labour councillor.

The embarrassed Byers said last night, "It was a terrible mistake. I had a few drinks at the bar and, before I knew it, I was involved in an unseemly socks act."

He continued, "Yes, I admit it. It was a case of unprotected socks, as I did not have my shoes on at the time."

Nude Labour

Labour colleagues said, "This is the end for Byers. It is one thing to mess up the railways and lie to Parliament. But it is quite another to be caught in a sordid socks scandal *(cont. p. 94)*

POETRY CORNER

**In Memoriam
Inspector Morse (aka
John Thaw)**

So. Farewell then
John Thaw,
Known to millions
As Inspector
Morse.

"Lew-is!" That was
Your catchphrase.

Many readers have pointed out
The uncanny prescience of
My last poem
When I asked "Who
Will be the next TV detective
To go
After Stratford Johns
(Inspector Barlow
Of Z Cars fame)
And Barry Foster
(Inspector Van der Valk)?"

Dit-dit-dit
Da-da-da
Dit-dit-dit
That was your theme tune.

Whereas Barlow's was
Da-da-da
Di-dum-dum-dum-dum
And Van der Valk's
Was
Da-da-da-da
Dadada
Da-da-da-da-da,
As I pointed out
In my last two
Poems.

Endeavour J. Thribb (17½)

**In Memoriam
Call My Bluff,
long-running BBC quiz
programme**

So. Farewell then
Call My Bluff.
Finally, they have called
Yours.

E.J. Thribb

Thribb. Is it:

a) *a South American monkey?*

b) *a type of pewter bowl used
in Anglo-Saxon burial
ceremonies?*

c) *a poet and eulogist whose
new selection of verses* A
Funeral Garland For Her
Majesty Queen Elizabeth The
Queen Mother *has just been
published?*

*"Your house is fine – you don't need any chemical
damp-proofing anywhere"*

*"I won't bother you now – you're obviously on your
way to work"*

"Put your shirt on, mate!"

**In Memoriam
Punch, a magazine
(1841-1992; 1996-2002)**

So. Farewell then
Al Fayed's money.
(Surely Punch?)

After six years
You have
Died
For the
Second time.

What will they put
On your gravestone?

"Not dead but
Only sleeping."

Like your readers.

All six of
Them.

E.J. Thribb (£17½ million
down the drain)

**Lines on the 100th
anniversary of Marmite**

So.
Marmite.
Congratulations.

You are
100.

Famous spread
On toast.
Enjoyed by
Millions.

But what
Is it made of?

Perhaps we
Shall never
Know.

E.J. Thribb (17½)

**Lines on the Retirement
of Russell Twisk,
Editor of the Reader's
Digest**

So. Farewell
Then Russell
Twisk.

Twisk.
It is a
Strange name.

A cross
Between whisk
And twist.

E.J. Thrisk (17½)

In Memoriam Baron Hans Thyssen Bornemisza de Kaszon, Art Collector, Ruth Handler, Creator of the Barbie Doll, and General Alexander Lebed, Russian war hero

So. Farewell
Then
All three
Of you.

It is true
What they say –
People always
Die in threes.

You remember
Inspector Morse,
Van der Valk and
The Z-Cars man.*

Or, more recently,
Spike Milligan,
Barry Took
And Dudley Moore.

But, strangely,
You three had
Nothing in common.
            E.J. Thribb (17½)

* *The Editor writes:* Due to lack of space it was not possible to include Mr Thribb's verbal renditions of the relevant theme tunes – e.g. Z-Cars (Da-da-da-di-dum-dum-dum-dum-dum), Inspector Morse (Dit-dit-dit-da-dot-dot-dot) and Van der Valk (Da-da-da-da-da-da-da-da-da etc). We apologise for any disappointment to our readers.

In Memoriam Lord Hailsham

So. Farewell
Then.
Lord Hailsham.
Formerly Quintin
Hogg.

Famous for
Ringing a bell
Once at a Tory
Conference.

Now the Bell
Has tolled
For you.

As we say
In *Private Eye*.
Not Continued
Age 94.
            E.J. Thribb

Scenes You Seldom See

"Ben's not very bright for his age"

"I'll call you back – this conversation is really annoying people"

"Actually, things are a lot better nowadays than they were in my day"

Lines on the Retirement of Arthur Scargill as Life-President of the National Union of Mineworkers

So. Farewell then
Arthur Scargill,
Famed militant leader of
Britain's miners.

With your
Combed-over hair
And high-pitched
Yorkshire voice,
You were the image
Of the 1970s.

"Everybody out!"
Yes, that was your
Catchphrase.
And now you are.

Although you
Were life-president
You are not dead.
Although the same
Cannot be said
For your
Union.
            E.J. Thribb,
    Life President of the National
    Union of Poetical Obituarists
    (NUPO). Membership: one.

In Memoriam Sir Gerald Whent, founder of Vodafone

So. Farewell
Then
Sir Gerald Whent,
Founder of
Vodafone.

What an ideal
Name for someone
Who has died.

Your successor
Is called Sir
Christopher Gent.

"Whent
And Gent".

Who says I
Cannot write poetry
That
Rhymes?
            E.J. Thribb (£17½ billion
                    in the red)

This poem is sponsored by VodaGnome

77

COUGH: MIXTURE AS BEFORE

by Our Political Staff Peter O'Bore

IN A FURTHER dazzling initiative which has thrown a bombshell into the normally placid world of Westminster, Mr Duncan Cough, leader of the Conservative Party, has let it be known that he proposes to say nothing about anything for the indefinite future.

When asked last night to comment on his new "no comment" policy, Cough cleverly refused to comment.

A close friend of Mr Cough said, "You won't catch him out that way. He's far too bright for you lot."

Sources in Tory Central Office said, "Iain's strategy is really paying off. Our private polling shows that 86% of the voters have no idea who he is. In May the figure was only 73%. The message is getting across – don't blame the Tories, because you've forgotten who we are."

Oliver Letwin is 23.

'NO' CAMPAIGN GATHERS MOMENTUM

by Our Economics Staff **Euro Geller**

AFTER a much-heralded launch last week, the Euro campaign to say "no" to celebrities has been attracting enormous support across the country.

"It's not political," said a typical anti-celebrity campaigner. "It's just that we don't want celebrities foisted on us when we have no say in the matter."

Said another, "There is no evidence that there are any benefits to having celebrities. And I think that in the long term they are probably damaging to our British way of life.

"We've managed without celebrities running our economy for thousands of years. Now, whether we like it or not, we suddenly have comedians telling us about convergence theory."

He concluded: "It's time we had a referendum on the celebrity issue and finally allow the nation to say 'no' to these people off the telly."

On Other Pages

☐ Little and Large on the crisis in British pensions **2**

☐ Keith Harris and Orville on a possible return to the Gold Standard **3**

☐ Adolf Hitler on why one should not laugh at Rik Mayall **94**

'WE ARE ALL RACISTS'
Says Sir David Calvert-Twitte

by Our Home Affairs Staff **Ray Cyst**

THE HEAD of Britain's new-look Crown Prosecution Service told reporters today, "We are all racists now, particularly in my department. I see a white man and I immediately assume he is a bigot. It is not something I'm proud of but it is just the way I'm made. I tend to pick on white people and blame them when things go wrong – which they do all the time when I'm in charge. If only I was a black man then I'd be much better at my job."

Sir David's views were given on Radio 4's popular interview programme *On The Make* with John Humphrys.

Summer Walks
with Old Bruce Anderson

No. 94
The Garvaghy Road

SEE traditional Northern Ireland in all its midsummer glory as you walk down this picturesque street strewn with rocks and burnt-out cars. If you listen carefully, you can hear the sound of marching bands, and if you are very lucky, you will hear the coarse cry of the Orange-Crested Paisley with his traditional call "Fockdapope! Fockdapope! Fockdapope!"

Assemble at nine o'clock with a stout pair of walking shoes, a bowler hat and an armour-plated vest. Survivors to meet up at the Ulster Royal Infirmary at the end of the walk.

LIVINGSTONE SPEAKS OUT ON MMR

I prefer a single jab...

...and then, when they're winded, I push them off the wall

"Childline? I'm worried about my pension shortfall"

MAX HASTINGS

Now that you've given up being the editor of the Evening Standard, do you find you have more time to devote to things such as spoons?

I certainly have more time for a whole lot of things I enjoy. Fishing. Shooting. Fishing. There's nothing I enjoy more than standing up to my waist in a fast-flowing trout stream like the Test or the Itchen...

I'm sorry to bring you back to spoons. Would they have any part in your shooting and fishing?

That's a bloody stupid question, if I may say so. When trying to land a 20lb salmon, a spoon is the very last thing you'd think about.

You've also written a number of books about the war. Do you remember any part that was played by spoons in those events?

I don't know if you've actually read any of my books, but if you had, I think you'd realise what a bloody silly question that is.

But surely, every soldier would have carried a spoon in his knapsack?

He may have done. But I have to say there are rather more important issues at stake in a great battle than whether or not Tommy Atkins has got a spoon in his kitbag.

So that's another silly question is it?

You've taken the words right out of my – hang on a tick, I've just seen a pheasant out of the window asking to be shot. I know it's out of season, but I'm not having him digging up my nasturtiums. BANG. And if you put that in your damn fool interview I'll shoot you as well. And while you're asking about my new book, it's called The Art of Leadership With Rod and Gun, available in all good bookshops at £45.

Has anything amusing ever happened to you in connection with a spoon?

That's another bloody idiotic question.

NEXT WEEK: Simon Schama – *"Me And My Corkscrew."*

BUSH DECLARES WAR ON FRAUD

People fiddling figures is unacceptable... unless it's my brother in Florida

POLLY FILLER

ON HER NEW NOVEL

WHEN I wrote the first Polly Filler column I had no idea that within such a short time it would be a nationwide success, the subject of countless dinner party conversations, and of course a best-selling book and forthcoming film.

But maybe I should have known. From day one, grateful women have written to me saying, "Polly, you speak for working mothers everywhere. You tell it like it is. Your childcare problems are our childcare problems. Your useless partner is our useless partner. Your attempts to combine a fantastically successful career with being a supermum are just like ours –

although obviously we are not as good at it as you!!"

Clearly, I had tapped in to a national nerve. I had disovered the essential truth about women that no one had dared to tell before. They have jobs and children as well!!

The rest is history. And now, as my new novel hits the street, I still find the working women of Britain want to know the answer to one simple question: "Where did you find your nanny?" *(Surely "Where did you find the time to write this brilliant analysis of contemporary women's issues?" Ed.)*

OF COURSE, it's not as easy as it looks. Try telling your energetic and very bright toddler that you can't read him a bedtime story because you've got to finish the chapter in which your heroine can't read her toddler a bedtime story because she's working late!!! Don't talk to me about guilt!!

But I know it's all been worth it when I receive the sackfuls of letters and hordes of e-mails thanking me for my unique insights and telling me how marvellous I am.

But remember, girls. We're *all* marvellous, not *just* me. And that's the whole point.

Polly Filler's new novel "How Do You Fill That Column?" is available directly from www.remainders.com.uk

The Little Match Girl
by Hans Arthur Andersen

IT WAS terribly cold and it was the last day of the financial year. Conditions were perfect for selling matches and the Little Match Girl had sold over ten million matches on that very day, declaring pre-tax profits of over $50 billion dollars. Unfortunately she caught a cold and died and when the regulator investigated the accounts of matchgirl.com, they realised it had all been a fairytale and I was arrested.

© Hans Arthur Andersen

HOW U.S. BUSINESS WORKS

Sell!

Sell!

Cell!

"Look out! Accountant!"

COUGH: NO EASY MEDICINE

by Our Political Staff Peter O'Bore

IAIN DUNCAN COUGH, leader of the Conservative Party, last night refused to comment on Gordon Brown's spending review.

Friends of Mr Cough explained that the Tory leader hoped to discredit Mr Brown by saying nothing about the huge increases in public spending.

Said the friend, "It would be all too easy for Iain to come out and attack Mr Brown for being reckless and profligate. But how much cleverer it is to keep very quiet until everyone realises what a mess Mr Blair's government is making of everything."

A Liberal Democrat spokesman meanwhile attacked Mr Duncan Cough for stealing his party's policies.

"It was Charles Kennedy who first thought of the idea that a party leader should say nothing about anything, and the Tories have just copied it."

"We want to be divorced in church"

Radio Highlights

WHAT YOU MISSED

The Today Programme

Ed Stourton *(for it is he)*: And now, live from Madrid, we have Her Excellency Donna Anna della Paella, the Foreign Minister of Spain. Donna Anna, your country has just invaded Parsley Island, on the grounds that it belongs to Spain even though it is right next to Morocco. Why is this different from the situation over Gibraltar?

Paella: What a ridiculous question. The two situations could not be more different. Spain has a historic right to Parsley Island because its inhabitants all voted...

Stourton: ...don't you mean "goated"?

Paella: Please be quiet when I am talking. All of the goats on Parsley Island wish to be Spanish. And we have a sacred duty to protect their rights.

Stourton: Is this what we call the "Nanny State"?

Paella: You shuddupya face.

Stourton: But if these goats want to be Spanish, as you say, surely the people of Gibraltar want to be British?

Paella: No. This only shows you know nothing about history. The wishes of the people of Spain are quite clear on this issue. They want to have Gibraltar and they want to have the Isla Parsleya. This is what we call democracy, Mr Stourton. Perhaps it is time that you English began to learn what the word means.

Stourton: Thank you, Your Highness. And now, Thought For The Day, with the Chief Scientologist, Mr N. Ron Hubbard Jr.

Hubbard: When I was living on the Planet Bargon 300 million years ago, the thought struck me that *(Cont. 94kHz)*

No. 94 The Signing of Magna Carta

In the summer of 2002 AD, in a historic ceremony at the Field of Runnyscared, King Blunkett I, accompanied by his faithful dog Griswold, received in audience the most powerful barons of the kingdom – the Baron Black, the Baron Desmond the Dirty and the Baron Rothermere, accompanied by his trusty squire Dacre.

The Lords of Middle England set out their demands, that all the villeins and miscreants should be strung up, for, quoth they, "Such be the onlie tongue they comprehendeth."

And King Blunkett agreed to their every demand, right down to their insistence on the instant banishment of the poor asylum-seekers who had come to Britain's shores seeking social security and free council housing. Such was his fear of the all-powerful barons.

Extract from The Simon Schama "History of Britain Experience".

New Greetings Cards No. 94

The Times
and Universal Register

1 penny

Ratings For Big Bedlam Soar

Ye most popular entertainment of ye moment in ye Metropolis is ye Big Bedlam Showe, presented by the celebrated showmen Mr Julian Bellamy and Mr Peter Bazalgette.

Each night vast queues form of excited gentlefolke, anxious to witnesse with their own eyes ye sad anticks of ye unfortunate and mentally disturbed wretches who dwell within ye house of Bedlam.

Ye poore inmates strip themselves naked, shriek with laughter and shout profanities at each other all ye nighte long.

On some nights, it hath been whispered abroade, the lunaticks even perform lewde acts with each other, much to ye entertainement of ye ladies and gentlemen viewing from ye safety of ye balconies.

Foremost among ye curiosities on display is ye now celebrated Mistress Jade, an uncomely wench of limited mental

powers, who hath been dubbed by ye hackes of Grubbe Street, namely Masters Yelland and Moron, as "Ye Pigge".

The hope of these bloodthirstie hackes is that the populace will rise up and murder Mistress Jade, thus adding greatlie to ye publick stocke of harmless pleasure.

Ye Stoppe Presse

Hundreds forced to walk to worke in Capital as ye sedan men "down chairs" in 24-hour strike **2**

His Majestie King George III is pleased to announce his bestowal of a knighthood on Dr Jonathan, ye celebrated savant **7**

Funny cartoon by Hogarth **94**

BLUNKETT TO ABOLISH LEGAL SYSTEM

by Our Legal Correspondent **Joshua Rosenbeard**

THE Home Secretary David Blunkett is planning the most radical reform of Britain's legal system since the Middle Ages by abolishing the age-old concept of 'the rule of law'.

"In a modern Britain," Mr Blunkett told MPs yesterday, "we don't need all the airy-fairy stuff about courts and juries and outdated notions such as 'innocence'."

Security Blunkett

"It is ludicrous," said the Home Secretary, "that in the 21st century the police cannot just put people in prison when

they are obviously guilty.

"Take the Stephen Lawrence case for example. OK, the police made a tremendous mess of it the first time round. But under my new system they will be given a second chance to mess it up again."

Britain's policemen last night welcomed Mr Blunkett's proposals.

Said Superintendent Knacker, spokesman for the Police Federation, "The idea of replacing the jury with twelve policemen is one we have been campaigning for for years. We are confident it will quickly lead to a massive increase in convictions, particularly if Mr Blunkett also agrees to replace judges with senior police officers."

"If you win Big Brother, are you enough of a celebrity to enter Celebrity Big Brother?"

Old Actor Dates Thin Actress

by **Harrison Broad and Skeleta Flockhart**

AN OLD actor was seen out today with a thin actress. "The fact that there is such a big gap between our weights is not a problem," said the thin actress. He is 15 stone and she is only 6 stone 3lb.

"We are very much in the newspaper," said the old actor.

THIS WEEK

BRIAN SEWELL

I don't suppose there are many modern spoons in your collection. Am I right?

You couldn't have said a truer word, even if you tried. The sheer vulgarity of modern design, not just of the humble spoon, but of all contemporary kitchen equipment, makes one despair.

What's your earliest memory of spoons?

I remember very vividly being taken to the Victoria & Albert Museum by my grandmother. It was a bitterly cold February morning and Exhibition Road was pure Sickert – the dark, brooding buildings against a threatening snow-filled sky...

Which brings us to the fascinating question of spoons in art...

Indeed. And fascinating it is. One of the great masterpieces of spoon painting hangs in the Musée de Napoléon in Limoges. The artist of this famous wood panel is generally believed to be Giovanni di Janini, but I think this attribution is profoundly mistake, as the work is much earlier, almost certainly by the Master of Antwerp.

I'm afraid I don't know the painting. Is it full of spoons?

No, of course not. No artist of any rank would paint a picture of a spoon, *per se*. This picture shows St Gervase offering a spoon to the infant Jesus. It's an overwhelming image and one that remains with one long after one is dead. Most modern art is a sort of pornography which is there to stimulate but does nothing else.

Has anything amusing ever happened to you in connection with a spoon?

Alas, no. Would that it had!

NEXT WEEK: Ann Widdecombe *"Me And My Frying Pan."*

Edinburgh Highlights

The six fringe hits you won't want to miss

by Our Arts Staff **Sue Dough**

Don Giovanni – Opera Norwich's reworking of the Mozart classic (Venue No. 42,734) sets it on board the QE2.

Theatre
Macbeth
St Columba's Caravan Park. Venue No. 738

ALL NUDE Ukranian production takes Shakespeare's masterpiece and sets it on the moon in the year 3037. An outstanding performance as Lady Macbeth by the acclaimed Serge Bonkov.

"A lunar tour de force" – Big Issue

Film
Moose!
The Ritzy. Venue 78,408

AWARD-WINNING Canadian director Annette de la Nougerede tells the story of a young Taliban asylum seeker who is befriended by two lesbian lorry drivers in a suburb of Quebec. Stars Hamad Hamas as himself.

"Heartwarming, magical cinema though perhaps seven hours was a little long" – Sheridan Morley

Jazz
Men with Beards
The Sad Café. Venue 9,336

ALL star line-up of men with beards including Chris Beaver, Ronnie Whiskers, Gary Goatee and new star Courtney Moustache.

"Mmmm… nice" – Beards and Beardsmen

Comedy
The Shorter Oxford English Dictionary Show
BT Phone and Internet Centre, The Royal Mile. Venue No. 3,712

TOP Irish stand-up Peter O' Touretz goes through the dictionary picking out the swear words.

"The endless repetition of expletives is both disturbing and hysterical" – Time Out

Dance
Les Trois Chiens de Limoges
Starbucks Café, Princes Street. Venue No. 979

AMAZING all-dog ballet company perform works by Bach, Wolfhound Mozart and Sir Harrison Dogwhistle.

"Ballet at its best" – Radio 3's Late Junction

Art
Orkney Visions
The Cartier Bresson Room, Caledonian Hotel. Venue 10,2473

Gritty black and white images of Orkney fisher folk, from the nineteen thirties to the present day, by one of Scotland's most neglected photographers Hamish MacApple.

"MacApple's landscapes have a resonance at once nostalgic and contemporary" – Woman's Hour *(That's enough Festival, Ed.)*

"There must be easier ways to release equity on the house"

POLLY FILLER

ON THE AUGUST NIGHTMARE

IT'S THE summer holidays and I am furious. The reason will be well-known to all you working mums and useless dads out there, and that is the old question, "Who is going to look after the children while we go on holiday?"

The answer should be simple. The nanny. Yet the sort of girls one is forced to employ nowadays refuse to work a 24-hour day for 3 weeks looking after the toddler Charlie whilst Simon and I go off for a week's scuba diving in Zanzibar, a week's ballooning in Madagascar and a week to flop around camel racing in Dubai.

Honestly! All we want is a little time together for the two of us, away from the stress of supervising Charlie's childcare and what happens?

A flat refusal from the ungrateful Angolan teenager!

SO THE next choice is obvious. The grandparents should do it. Surely one of these couples should be grateful for a chance to spend three weeks bonding with their grandson?

But no. My mother is too busy swanning about visiting my father in hospital and the useless Simon's parents are even more useless. They are dead.

So with no one willing to lift a finger to help us get away and recharge our batteries, what on earth were we supposed to do?

Stay at home? Take Charlie with us? Go stark staring mad?

Any readers who have any suggestions, do let me know!

© Polly Filler, all newspapers.

"Hi, I'm bored, can you come in and mess up the jumpers?"

LIVER GETS HUMAN TRANSPLANT

By Our Celebrity Staff
Philippa Redtop

A healthy liver was today given a new George Best, hospital authorities announced.

A spokesman for the transplanted organ told reporters "the operation has been a success, but the liver is furious".

"It was hoping to live out its days in a healthy human being, but now it finds it is facing years of abuse as part of the world's greatest living drunk" *(surely 'footballer'? Ed.)*.

Doctors warn that the liver may yet reject its new host and that it was too early to celebrate the success of the operation with a round of trebles.

Parenting

Exclusive to all newspapers

7 Fun Modern Ways To Entertain Your Children During The Summer Holidays

1. Tell them to play on their Gameboys
2. Tell them to play on their Playstations
3. Tell them to play on their mobile phones
4. Tell them to play on their computers
5. Tell them to watch television
6. Tell them to go to bed
7. Er...
8. That's it.

"It seems they're not as intelligent as we thought"

BIG BROTHER

Diana Fountain Controversy

It's shallow...

It's expensive...

It gushes...

It goes round in a circle...

It makes me weep...

It's loopy...

MEN IN GREEN (BELT)

I'm building more houses

Why? You've already got four

THAT NEWSNIGHT INTERVIEW YOU DIDN'T SEE

(Charles Kennedy talks to Jeremy Paxman)

Kennedy: So, Jeremy, glad to see you've sobered up enough to come on the show.

Paxman: I'm sorry...

Kennedy: I thought you might be lying on your own somewhere, unable to stand up...

Paxman: No, I...

Kennedy: So why aren't you married? Are you a poof?

Paxman: No, I'm not...

Kennedy: Alright then, it must be because you like a string of totty, don't you?

Paxman: No, no...

Kennedy: I've seen you ogling the female students on University Challenge. I bet that's not all you get up to! Whoar! Eh?!

Paxman: Really, I think I should...

Kennedy: So, how many bottles of whisky a day do you drink with these blonde bimbos? One, two... ten?

Paxman: And now a look at tomorrow's papers. They all seem to lead on this interview *(cont. p. 94)*

That Tony Benn Citation In Full

SALUTAMUS ANTONIUS BENNUS, QUONDAM WEDGWOODIBUS BENNISSIMO, DOMINUS STANSGATII, SED POPULARITER SOLE "TONIUS", TRIBUNUS PLEBORUM ET COMRADUS SOCIALISTICUS, FAMOSISSIMUS PER BIBENDO MUGGOS GIGANTICOS TYPHOONENSIS PGTIPOSQUE ET PUFFANDO PIPO NICOTINO MALODOROSIMO, SED ATQUE NOTABILE QUA MINISTERIUS TECHNOLOGICUS SUB PONTIFEX HAROLDUS WISLONIUS (MORTUS) ET AEDIFICAVIT COLUMNUM MONUMENTALIUM POSTOFFICUM IN LONDINIUM CUM RESTORANTE REVOLVANDO (NUNC FERMATUS PER DURATIONEM), SED ATQUE MILLIONIBUS VERBIS RECORDATUS IN "JOURNALIOS TONIUS BENNI" PUBLICATUS IN MILLE VOLUMIS INTERMINABILIS STUPENDUS BORUS ET SOMNIFERENTIUS, IN QUO CLAMAVIT "EGO SUM CORRECTUS SEMPER", OCULIS SWIVELLENTIUS ET BONKERIUS, SED NUNC THESPIANUS CELEBRATUS IN THEATRICALIS "UNOS HOMO SPECTACULUS" ADORATUS PER CLASSIBUS MEDIIS IN SUBURBES EG GUILDFORDIUM, CROYDONICUS ET WELLUS TUNBRIDGIENSIS, BOOKITE QUAM CELERRIME UT EVADERE DISAPPOINTIMENTUM. SALUTAMUS SENEX SPARTICUS MAXIMUS.

© UNIVERSITATE PAISLEYENSIS (QUONDAM HAMILTONIUS ACADEMICALIS)

'YES, I AM USELESS' Admits Top Tory

by Our Political Staff **Matthew Gay-Paree**

THE WORLD of Westminster was rocked to its foundations last night when a senior Conservative, Mr Alan Duncan Smith, admitted in an interview that he was "useless" and had been for years.

"For a long time," he said, "I tried to keep it secret. But then I realised that things had changed and that in the 21st century it was perfectly acceptable to be useless and to be a politician.

"Labour have realised this for years, and have been prepared to promote lots of useless people up to Cabinet level.

"It is time that the Tories realised that it is no longer a stigma to be useless, and that a lot of well-known Tories have been useless without it hindering their careers.

Jeremy Thorpedo

"I think people's attitudes really have changed. An old lady in my constituency came up to me the other day and said, 'Alan, I always suspected that you were useless. But now that you have come out and admitted it, I really admire your bravery.' "

Alan Duncan Smith is 37.

"Can't talk now, I'm chatting"

Eye Probe

PAST TORIES: Were They Useless?

Edward Heath
There were repeated rumours around Westminster during his premiership that he was useless, but he has never publicly admitted it.

Michael Portillo
Knowing that many journalists were on his trail and were about to expose him for being useless, he "outed" himself and gave up politics.

William Hague
Tearoom gossip pointed the finger at Hague for being useless, but it was only after he had lost the 2001 election that he confessed to his problem.

Baroness Thatcher
Few would ever have dared to suggest that she was useless, with the exception of Edward Heath, who may have been using this tactic as a screen to hide his own uselessness.

"Your chariot of fire has arrived"

COUGH GETS WORSE

by Our Tory Staff **Peter O'Bore**

STUNG by criticism that he has done absolutely nothing since being elected leader of the Conservative Party last September, Mr Iain Duncan Cough last night shocked his three remaining supporters by sacking party chairman David Whohe while he was on holiday in Florida fishing for votes in the next leadership election *(Surely 'marlin'? Ed.).*

Unfortunately, Mr Whohe was unaware of Mr Cough's shock initiative because his mobile telephone was not working, but on his return to Gatwick he read that he had been fired in an old copy of the Daily Mail.

Mr Whohe immediately rang Duncan Cough at his luxury Berkshire hideaway, Strepsils, to ask what was going on.

Mr Cough sprang into action once again and told him that, despite having sacked Mr Whohe the day before, he would now like to promote him to the key job of trying to work out what John Prescott is saying.

In a statement issued later to the press, Mr Cough said, "It is quite untrue to say that I sacked Mr Whohe and replaced him with Mrs Whoshe. Even if I did, I want to make it clear that I have such confidence in Mr Whohe's loyalty and commitment that I promise to back him when he stands against me for the leadership next week."

Mr Oliver Letwin is 22.

A Taxi Driver Writes

Every week a well-known cab driver is invited to comment on an issue of topical importance.

THIS WEEK:
Normo Tebbs
(cab no. 764321) on Homosexuality in the Conservative Party.

Gor blimey! See all that fuss about the Tory shirtlifter? Who gives a toss! What 'e does in his private life is his business, or maybe just his psychiatrist's ha ha ha! No, no. Live and let live, that's what I say obviously but them Tories are finished unless they get back to the real issues that the punters are interested in – ie, whether poofs should be strung up. I mean, it's the only language they understand, isn't it? Same with all them Muslim lesbian asylum seekers – you know the type, guv.

I 'ad that Simon Heffer in the back of the cab once. Very clever man.

SADDAM AGREES TO HAND OVER WEAPONS OF MASS DESTRUCTION

ENGLAND TRIUMPH

by Our Athletics Staff **PHILIPPA SPORTS-SECTION**

THE 38,000 capacity crowd in Manchester's sunlit Stadium of Glory rose to their feet screaming in rapture yesterday to salute the astonishing world-class performance of plucky Moss-side-born local lass Michelle Yelland, 24, as she gallantly powered in with a personal best time of only 3 hours 33 minutes, to take a stunning fourth place in the 20,000 metres Synchronised Underwater Hurdles.

After the race, Michelle told the BBC's Sally Jockstrap, "This is the most fantastic moment in my life. I always dreamed that one day I could come fourth in a race like this and now I have.

"Fortunately, the three African runners were so far ahead of me that I didn't have to think about them during the race."

As the crowd hummed Land of Hope and Glory under its breath during the playing of the Kenyan national anthem, Michelle performed a lap of honour, but unfortunately was forced to retire halfway round, due to a recurrence of her old hamstring problem.

Results

20,000 Metre Synchronised Underwater Hurdles: 1, C. Kipcat (Kenya); 2, J. Kipcat (Kenya); 3, K. Kipcat (Kenya); 4, M. Yelland (England); 5,6,7,8, Who cares?
400 Metre Men's Jacuzzi: 1, F. Montgomery-Jarvis (New Zealand); 2, P.W.B. McCready (Canada); 3, Fletcher Christian (Pitcairn); 94, Dwayne Slomo (England)
Men's One-Legged Freestyle Groping: 1, Bruce Blimey (Aus)
(That's enough Commonwealth Games. Ed.)

Why are English men so pathetic?

asks Leah McLaren

SHE'S YOUNG, attractive and Canadian. Yet, after a dozen attempts, Leah McLaren could not find one male editor in this country who could resist publishing her article.

"What is wrong with them all?", asked Liah McLaren. "I made it perfectly clear that this was really thin stuff, but every single one of them fell for it".

Leah McItallup said that her terrible experiences have taught her some very important lessons about English editors.

1. The ones who have been to boarding schools like Eton are the worst – Boris Johnson, for example, was too scared of women to say, "No thanks, this is rubbish."

2. English editors always split the bill so that they all end up paying for the same piece by me.

3. English editors are all repressed heterosexuals who are dying to put in a picture of a blonde girl with a story about sex.

4. English editors all drink too much – they must do to have printed such ropy old drivel.

© *All newspapers, every day*

"Bad dog!"

DANDO CASE: POLICE FOUND INNOCENT

by Our Dando Staff **Desperate Dando**

IN A SHOCK verdict, the Appeal Court yesterday ruled that the police were wholly vindicated in their desire to find someone guilty of shooting a famous television personality.

The judges were unanimous that the case brought by the police against Mr Barry George had been "overwhelming".

"The task in front of these dedicated officers was colossal," said Lord Justice Cocklecarrot.

"Having arrested Mr Boy George for this heinous crime, they were then in the unenviable position of having no evidence on which to convict him.

"But justice was not to be denied. After labouring night and day for months on end, they finally came up with the clinching piece of evidence – a small scrap of paper bearing the incriminating words 'He must have done it because we arrested him' and bearing the signature of Inspector 'Knacker of the Yard' Knacker, head of the 5000-strong 'Find the Dando Killer' unit."

Speaking outside the courtroom after the verdict, Inspector Knacker told waiting newsmen, "This is a great day for British justice. I and my colleagues have been protesting for years that we were totally innocent, and now the British legal system has finally proved us right."

Inspector Knacker is 56.

Daily Mail

FRIDAY, AUGUST 9, 2002

GIANT ASTEROID WILL HIT EARTH AND END PROPERTY BOOM SHOCK

by Daily Mail Staff
Clare Monger

NEW LABOUR were left squirming yesterday as news emerged that a giant asteroid hurtling towards the earth at thousands of miles an hour could spell a premature end to the property boom some time in 2019.

A spokesman for the Conservative Party said: "Take it from me, when this huge lump of molten rock hits the planet's surface and destroys every living thing in its wake, the likes of Tony Blair and Gordon Brown will have egg all over their faces and they'll be forced to put their hands up and concede defeat."

On Other Pages Scientists say that awful hot weather was the fault of the Labour Government **2** Scientists say those awful storms that followed that awful hot weather were the fault of the Labour Government **3** Pictures of women in bikinis **4-94**

Nigel Dumpster

My Marriage to Duke's Daughter Has 'Broken Down'

■ I can reveal exclusively to readers of the Daily Mail that the marriage of top diary columnist, myself, 76, to Lady Camilla Dumpster, the third daughter of the 32nd Duke of Leeds and fourteenth cousin twice removed of her late Majesty, Queen Elizabeth the Queen Mother, has, sadly, irretrievably collapsed.

Close friends tell me that I am living apart from my wife, and that divorce proceedings are under way.

Sources close to myself have also revealed that I am being comforted by a young, nubile companion (surely "bottle of whisky"?) and that I am to be seen more and more frequently in the seedy environs of Chelsea, accompanied by my latest squeeze, who it seems has never had the good fortune to meet top billionaire Robert Sangster, 94.

Sad Times For Me

■ These marital difficulties come at a bad time for Sherborne-educated myself, as they coincide with my imminent court appearance at the celebrated magistrates court in London's fashionable Bow Street, where I am to face charges of so-called drunken driving.

In doing so, I will join a long and distinguished list of aristocrats and members of the Royal Family who have stood in the dock on motoring charges.

These include the Princess Royal, the Marquess of Blandford, who is heir to the 21st Duke of Marlborough, the late Marquess of Bristol and the Hon. Jacaranda Templeton-Twytte, 2nd cousin to the disgraced diarist and socialite, previously married to the 14th daughter of the 83rd Duke of Norfolk, myself.

Diarist Washed Up

■ Whatever has happened to myself, friends close to me were asking last night. Said one, "It's sad about Nigel. He's become the sort of figure he used to write about.

"No wonder the Mail is having to take on new recruits from other down-market rags in a desperate attempt to find some stories."

Myself is 74.

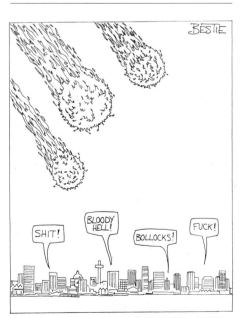

WHEN THE GREAT BALLS OF FIRE APPROACHED NOBODY SAID 'GOODNESS GRACIOUS'

(In memoriam Otis Blackwell, songwriter)

The Daily Telegraph

Est 1855

Full marks to the Mayor

This newspaper cannot disguise its relief that at last London has a truly right-wing mayor who is not afraid to run our capital city in the interests of the rich, at the expense of the poor. Mr Livingstone's courageous scheme has rightly earned him the sobriquet "Blue Ken".

The idea is breathtakingly simple. Those who can afford to pay Mr Livingstone's new congestion charge will be free to cruise around the empty streets of London, enjoying the privilege that their industry and enterprise has rightly earned. Meanwhile the working classes will quite rightly be forced to leave their cars and to squeeze their way onto antiquated buses and tubes, or the exciting new "standing-up only" cattle trucks provided by that excellent British Le Connex du Sud-Est.

It may be too early for "Blue Ken" to put himself forward as the next leader of the Conservative Party, but Mr Duncan Smith and his gay henchmen sshould be quaking in their boots.

On my bike

by
Beano Boris Johnson

Blimey! Yours truly was just taking a spin on his trusty old Raleigh Roadster (c.1955) when, woops, would you believe it, I became the first ever victim of that latest affliction of Islington's politically correct thought police, namely, a hatchet-faced woman on another bike pulling up next to me at the traffic lights and shouting at me, "That column of yours is absolute garbage – can't you find something more interesting to write about than how you cycle to work on your rotten bike?"

Cripes, talk about batey! What's a chap to do when he's been ticked off in no uncertain manner by someone even more frightening than Nanny?

© *The Daily Beano-graph*

NEW-LOOK QUEEN:
THEN AND NOW
No. 94: The Royal Tattoo

THEN

NOW

A SPOONERISM

GALLOWAY SHOCK

FILM CENSOR –
'Children Should Not Watch Pornography'

by Our Media Staff **P.G. Titz**

THE NEW film censor, Sir Quentin Thomas, has outraged the film business by suggesting that "young children should probably not watch sexually violent scenes on the screen".

Said one outraged spokesman for the cinema community, "This is a return to the dark ages before Andreas Whittam Stiff."

This was a reference to Sir Quentin Thomas' predecessor who was widely respected by film makers as a necessary liberalising force in their industry.

The spokesman continued, "Cinematic art needs the widest possible audience and to suggest that pornography is only suitable for so-called adults is a terrible restriction on the basic freedom of the artist to make as much money as *(cont. p. 94)*

Bores Demand Equal Time With Bores

by Our Religious Staff **A. Theist**

A HUNDRED of Britain's most heavyweight bores have petitioned the BBC for "equal access" to the Today programme's prestigious 'Bore of the Day' slot.

The bores include such well-known names as Sir Ludicrous Kennedy, Sir Harold Pinter, Dame Polly Toynbee and Professor Sir Richard Borekins.

Radio Bore

Says Sir Ludicrous, "It is outrageous that every day we are forced to listen to the mindless bletherings of the BBC's so-called God squad, such as the Chief Druid, the Bishop of Neasden and Pappadum Singh, when bores such as myself are kept off the air."

World-famous playwright Sir Harold Pinter OM said, "This censorship is worse than Hitler's Germany. They will be burning our plays next."

Sir Ludicrous is 106.

What You Won't Hear

Script for *Bore Of The Day* slot, written by **Harold Pinter**

Naughtie *(for it is he)*: And now, to present Bore For The Day, we are very honoured to welcome to the Today studio one of the greatest bores of all time, Dame Harold Pinter.

Pinter: You know, in a very real sense, when I heard the news that the imperialist warmonger Bush was planning a genocidal attack on that champion of human rights Saddam Hussein, I wrote a letter to the Guardian saying what a bastard he is.

(Two minutes of menacing silence)

Naughtie: And now over to Michael Fish for today's weather.

Fish: Hullo again *(cont'd. 94 kHz)*

The girls of St Crumpets celebrate record A-Level results. These four girls between them have got 500 Grade A*s. Said the Editor of the Daily Telegraph, "I am delighted for our readers that these girls are so attractive. It's a shame that they aren't showing more leg like Gwyneth Paltrow last Friday. Still phwoar, eh?"

COMING SOON IN THE EYE

'THE SECRET DIANA YOU NEVER KNEW'

by her former bodyguard KEN BROKE

IN THIS exclusive serial-isation we reveal the hitherto unknown secrets about the woman they called Princess of Hearts.

Did you know...

● **Diana was a neurotic woman who suffered from serious eating disorders.**

● **She was besotted by a married art dealer and once rang him 400 times in one evening.**

● **Diana did not love her husband whom she suspected of an affair with a married woman (believed to be Camilla Parker-Bowles).**

● **Er...**

● **That's it.**

In his position as the Princess's bodyguard, Broke was in a unique position to know her innermost thoughts and passions.

Now, in the public interest, he has decided to break his code of silence in order to make a lot of money *(Surely "tell it like it was"? Ed.)*

Revealed: Mother-in-law

St Cakes Delays Beginning of Term

By Our Education Staff **John Scare**

THE PRESTIGIOUS Midland independent boarding school St Cakes (Motto: Quis Paget Entrat – "Who Pays Gets In") has been forced to postpone the opening of Sodom Term due to the Government insistence on checks being run on staff by the Criminal Records Bureau.

Said Headmaster Mr Kipling, "These routine checks are a menace. All they do is reveal that most of my staff have criminal records. I will be forced to find replacements which will prove costly and time consuming. This is political correctness gone mad."

University Vacancies

(continued from p. 94)

CONTEMPORARY ASHTRAY DESIGN

University of Legoland (formerly Windsor Safari Park) P45, WHSMITH, ESSO, LUX

TXT MSSG STDS

Nokia University (formerly World of Toasters, Bracknell) ASAP, BLT, KPNUTS, IM4U

HISTORY OF THE BIRO

Toynbee University (formerly Toynbee Poly) PLJ, BOAC, FCUK

DAYTIME TV STUDIES

University of Life (formerly Your Lounge) BBC1, ITV2, C4, SKY

POPULAR PSYCHOLOGY

UNPOPULAR PSYCHOLOGY

BLAME YOUR PARENTS

BLAME YOUR-SELF

RGJ

The Daily Hellograph
and all other papers

The Nation Mourns

WORDS cannot begin to express... sense of grief... agony... stunned... numb community in tears... a single rose... coming to terms... agony... why oh why?... Parents' dignity... churches packed... every parent's worst nightmare... why? whole nation stunned... the news we all dreaded to hear... the longest night... agony of waiting... keep going, there's no other news (Ed.)... tiny village united in grief... a nation mourns... media intrusion (not us)... respect their privacy... media hampering police enquiries (not us)... life must go on... questions remain... why oh why?

On Other Pages

What has Gone Wrong With Us? by Melanie Phillips **94**

The Evil Gene That Lurks Within Us All by Dr Raj Persaud **95**

I Too Have Children by D.J. Hack **96**

Tasteless Cartoon by Mac **97**

PLUS All The Premiership Goals

THE SAD LONERS WHO PROBABLY DID IT

by Crime Staff **Hugh Dunnett**

Psychological profile... kept themselves to themselves... staring eyes... Jekyll and Hyde... tattoo... tortured background... Grimsby... fish factory... mad look... not much evidence to go on... almost certainly guilty... string 'em up.

Myra Hindley

"I met him on the Internet"

HUNTER

THE TIMETABLE OF TERROR

How Inspector Knacker Tracked The Killers

Monday
Knacker warns killers he has no leads to go on at this stage.

Tuesday
Knacker appeals to killers to give themselves up.

Wednesday
Knacker tells media "We have every hope they are still alive, but we are still looking for the killers."

Thursday
Knacker sets killers a deadline: "Ring me on my mobile by midnight, or you will get away with it," he warns.

Friday
Knacker of the Yard sent from London to replace village Knacker. Couple give themselves up.

Saturday
Couple charged. Knacker tells press, "This is a triumph for good old-fashioned policing."

Grief As Story Ends

by Our Media Staff **Sally Season**

THERE was an overwhelming sense of shock and loss last night as journalists and editors alike were coming to terms with the news that the story was finally over.

Said one, "Nothing prepared us for the moment when we knew the story was no longer with us. Now we will have to rebuild our lives, by filling pages with pictures of celebrities with no clothes on!"

On other pages

Pictures of celebrities with no clothes on.

Exclusive to all papers

GHOULS MUST LEAVE VILLAGE

THIS nation must hang its head in shame today after it was revealed by the people of Soham that 'ghouls' were hanging around the village making it impossible for the community to return to any sort of normality.

The locals say these sick individuals have been spotted taking pictures outside the families local church, scribbling down notes outside the family home and incredibly, some have even been so callous as to stop mourners leaving services in a vain attempt to speak to them.

Whoever these twisted individuals are, we demand they leave the village immediately.

On Other Pages

Exclusive Pictures of Soham Church Service **4-17**

'Leave Me Alone,' says Weeping Mourner Leaving Church Service in exclusive interview **18-43**

'Bring Back Hanging for Ghouls' says no-one **44-57**

DID YOU GRIEVE ENOUGH?

A Daily Gnome probe to see if *you* are really caring

❶ How many hours have you wept in the light of recent tragedies and anniversaries of tragedies?
a) One
b) Three
c) More

❷ How many minutes silence for something did you observe yesterday?
a) One
b) Three
c) Still observing

❸ How many books of condolence have you signed this week?
a) None
b) One
c) Twenty four and over

❹ How many copies of the Daily Gnome's "A Nation Mourns Again" supplement have you bought?
a) Two hundred
b) Three hundred
b) Less than this because I am a mean uncaring callous bastard who is not fit to live in society and call myself a human being.

£1 MILLION REWARD

THE EXPRESS is offering a million-pound reward to itself if any members of the public would like to buy the newspaper and increase its sales.

If you even think that you might want to buy this sort of newspaper, then that could be vital information for our marketing department. We suspect that putting in blanket coverage of the recent horrific murders in Soham will lead to more readers. But we cannot be sure.

Only *you* can help us to find the truth. And £1 million will be our reward.

● **Call Express Newspapers at once and hear the coroner denounce us for interfering in a police inquiry.** *(Surely "Tell us what you like about the new Daily Excess"? Ed.)*

"I strongly advise a biscuit tin under your bed"

Mog to be 'put to sleep'

By Our Literary Editor
Cat Adie

Lord Mogg

THE MUCH-LOVED children's character created by Rupert Murdoch is to be "put to sleep" after a lifetime of putting other people to sleep. *(Surely 'entertaining children of all ages from ninety to ninety-five'? Ed.)*

The forgetful Mog has featured in hundreds of charming stories, including "Mog And The Importance Of The Gold Standard", "Mog And The Imminent Return Of The Ice Age", "Mog And The Upside-Down Graph", "Mog Has Lunch At The Garrick", "Mog Has Lunch At The Garrick Again", and "Mog Remembers Diana".

Said creator Mr Murdoch, "Mog has had a good run, and has delighted several generations of fans with his good natured incompetence. But we now feel that in the 21st century it is time to move on."

Lord Mogg is 106.

Is The Telegraph Getting Too Thin?

Asks Liz Hurley

EVER since I gave birth to a new baby I have noticed that the Daily Telegraph has been getting thinner and thinner.

Once a heavyweight newspaper, it is now looking dangerously waif-like and reports suggest that it has been on a desperate non-stop diet of pieces about myself.

This is not enough to sustain a healthy newspaper and if the Telegraph continues in this fashion, shedding readers, it could collapse and *(cont. p. 94)*

(cont. p. 94)

On Other Pages

Earth Summit Latest – Starving Millions Lose Weight Too **94**

"These days, all the people the bride has slept with sit this side – and all the people the bridegroom has slept with sit that side"

9/11
ONE YEAR ON

2000 of the world's most famous people remember where they were and what they were doing

SIR CHARLES POWELL

I was lunching at the Garrick with a very important person, i.e. myself, when I received a message that something pretty serious had happened in America. I immediately put a call through to some other very important people, and we all agreed that we should go off and watch the television to find out what was going on.

CONDOLEEZZA RICE-KRISPY

I was in my office in the White House when the telephone rang and someone said, "You should put on the television." When I was what was happening, I immediately rang the President to tell him to watch the television, but I was told that he was too busy watching television to take my call.

SIR EDWARD HEATH

I was giving lunch in Salisbury to a group of Chinese businessmen, whom I was entertaining with my celebrated recording of the Elgar Cockayne Overture. In the middle of the performance a member of my staff entered the room and suggested that I should switch on the televison. I quite rightly told him that I had rather more important things to do.

CHRIS PATTTEN

I was having a series of very important meetings with senior members of the European Commission to discuss our new Single European Fish Initiative, and a number of very interesting views had been put forward, particularly by the Luxembourg minister for posts and telecommunications. At this point I had a call from my old friend John Major, to say that he had switched on the television to watch the final of the NatWest Trophy, only to find that a terrible disaster had happened. I had to inform my colleagues and we then agreed to adjourn the meeting and watch the television.

SUE MACGREGOR

Unfortunately I was fast asleep having done the Today programme, which always meant that I had to get up at 3 o'clock in the morning in order to be at White City in time for our first editorial meeting which was always promptly at 4.30. Unfortunately on this occasion a really major disaster took place in the afternoon, well after the Today programme had gone off the air.

OSAMA BIN LADEN

I was in my cave shooting my latest video when someone rang on my mobile to tell me I should be watching the televison.

● Extracted from the specially commissioned 14-part Radio Four series *9/11: One Year On*, presented by Edward Stourton – "Radio's Mr Posh".

BUSH AND CHURCHILL
What They Have In Common

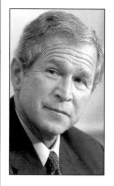

by Our World War Three Staff
Sir John Keegan, Bruce Anderson-Shelter and **Simon Hefferlump**

1. They are both world leaders.
2. They both have the initial Dubya.
3. They have both rid the world of an evil tyrant with a moustache, except Bush.
4. Er...
5. That's it.

That Earth Summit Menu in full

Waffle

– ✳ –

Tripe

– ✳ –

Baloney

– ✳ –

Junket

– ✳ –

Greens (off)

To drink: *No water*

BUSH EVOKES CHURCHILLIAN SPIRIT

BECKHAM IN NAME SHOCK

> Why did they keep calling her *Push?*

Theroux The Looking Glass

"Let me join you, Alice – I'm not just a journalist, I'm a friend..."

Daily Mail

COMMENT

A Disgraceful Act of Treachery

THERE IS nothing more sickening than the sight of this middle-aged man cynically making money by peddling treasonable tittle-tattle about the late Princess Diana.

What makes it worse is the spurious moral justification offered by this traitor that his seedy revelations are somehow in the public interest.

And how dare he suggest that the young princes would benefit from reading such tawdry rubbish about their mother.

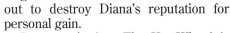

The fact is that this grubby muck-raker is a national disgrace who has set out to destroy Diana's reputation for personal gain.

But enough of me. That Ken Wharfe is pretty awful too.

© *All other newspapers as well*

On Other Pages

ANNE LAZILY's Brilliant New Series "Diana: Five Thousand Words On" – **7, 8, 9, 10**

"We don't want to know about Diana's vibrator, thank you" says **PHIL SPACE** – **11, 12, 13, 14**

"It's time to let her rest in peace" says **PHILLIPA PAGE – 14, 15, 16, 17, 18, 19, 20**

POLICE CARNIVAL – A HUGE SUCCESS

By Our Crime Staff **Phil Streets**

EUROPE'S largest police carnival was this year voted "a greater success than ever", as more than 100,000 members of the Metropolitan Police paraded through the streets of London's Notting Hill over the Bank Holiday weekend.

Members of the public were delighted at the spectacle of London's entire police force, arrayed in their colourful blue uniforms, laughing, singing and dancing through the streets.

Many of the officers joked with the crowd in their distinctive street-wise patois, with such quips as "watch it, sonny", and "we know where you live".

Carnival of the Pigs

After the eight-hour-long parade of the uniformed policemen came a more informal display as plain-clothes detectives wandered through the crowd disguised as Rastafarians, drug-peddlers and trans-sexual limbo dancers.

Said Inspector "Knacker of the Yard" Knacker, "It was a great day – only marred by the fact that there was no one to arrest."

"But all the lads had a very good overtime."

ME AND MY SPOON

THIS WEEK

NEIL KINNOCK

I suppose now you're Vice- President of the European Commission you have a lot of spoons from different countries?

Now, look, let's be totally frank and utterly honest about this. If you're trying to suggest that in any way I have used my position as a commissioner to get more spoons than I was legally entitled to, can I just make it absolutely clear that I totally repudiate and repudiate totally any suggestion whatsoever, and I know how you people work, with your anti-European smears and innuendoes, no, no, don't try to deny it, I know that you'd like everyone to believe that everyone in Europe is just out for themselves, with their snouts in the trough, trying to grab as many spoons as they can get their hands on, well, let me tell you that everything you are insinuating is a tissue of total travesties, and that there is not a shred of evidence, not one shred, to support the allegation that I, in my capacity as Fraud Commissioner, have in any way sought to increase my totally legitimate and permissible spoons allowance, which currently, I might add, is a very modest 306.85 Euro-spoons per annum (equating to 203.7 standard British spoons under the weighted transfer system), where was I, no, let me finish, you've had your say, which incidentally was totally disgraceful and a gross abuse of the freedom of the press, which incidentally I wholly and utterly support, so long as it is not irresponsibly used to promote an outrageous and wholly indefensible "Little Englander" agenda by trying to smear myself and my colleagues, who are as dedicated and hard-working *(Mr Kinnock continued in this vein for several hours, until the interviewer finally managed to ask him whether anything amusing had ever happened to him in connection with spoons, to which he replied "No, but" and continued for several more hours.)*

NEXT WEEK: Sally Gunnell on *"Me And My Bedside Alarm Clock."*

Forbidden Alliance

by Dame Sylvie Krin

THE STORY SO FAR: It is five years since Diana died, and so much has changed in Charles's world. Now read on..

"IT REALLY is appalling!" Charles threw down the Review section of the Sunday Times in disgust, and addressed the empty breakfast room at Highgrove.

"Why do they have to keep printing this rubbish year after year?"

There it was in black and white. The whole sordid story of his marriage to Diana, raked over yet again.

The tantrums. The traumas. The flagrant infidelities. The whole ghastly business.

And now her former bodyguard had joined in, repeating again every last drop of poisonous tittle-tattle from the "years of torment", as he had come to think of them.

He looked at the 18th century Ernst and Saunders longcase clock and saw that it was only 10.30. Perhaps a little too early in the day for what his father called "a snifter".

"But why not?" he thought. After all, his great-great-grandfather would have got through a whole case of champagne by this time of the morning.

He strode determinedly across the room to the solid gold drinks cabinet built in the shape of the Taj Mahal, a wedding present from the Emir of Tat, and poured himself a stiff shot of McHackey's Old Grouse.

As the potent restorative coursed through his veins, Charles began to feel more at ease with the day.

He looked musingly out of the window as the golden light of late summer slanted over the impeccably manicured organic lawns and caught the leaves of the great bulimia tree as they turned from verdant green to an autumnal amber.

"That's how life is," he thought. The hot storms of summer giving way to the calm, reflective tranquillity of autumn.

As his old friend and mentor Sir Laurens van der Post had put it so succinctly while they were sitting round the campfire in the Matahari Desert, "Life begins at 50." How true that was, how very, very true.

And how fortunate he was that all that ghastly period of his earlier life was now receding into the distant past.

The memories came flooding back. What a fool he had been!

He should have known from the start what it would be like, from the day Diana moved in and threw all his cherished Goon Show LPs into the wastepaper basket.

That's how their marriage had been, right up to the day it ended. She had glorified in defying him in everything she did.

He could almost hear her mocking voice now, echoing down the years.

"I don't care what you say, Charles! I shall do whatever I want. You can't tell me what to do. You're not even King..."

"YOU CAN'T tell me what to do. You're not even King!" The commanding presence of his beloved, Camilla, stood before him in blood-spattered jodhpurs and muddy riding boots, her face flushed from a long day in the saddle with the Earl of Cirencester's foxhounds.

She took a long defiant drag on a Goldman and Sachs full-strength cigarette, well knowing how annoyed he would be at her flagrant breach of his "no smoking in my presence" rule.

"Now look here, Camilla," he coughed, as the billows of acrid smoke assailed his sensitive royal nostrils. "If you go on this Countryside March thingie, you've no idea what an awkward position it would put me in.

"The tabloids would have my guts for garters," he explained. "I mean, they'll say that I gave you permission to go, and that I was endorsing the whole political, you know, thingie..."

Camilla tapped impatiently on an ample thigh with her Butler and Sloss riding crop.

"I don't need your permission to do anything, Charles!" she shouted. "We're not even married, in case you hadn't noticed.

"And when did you ever worry about interfering in politics? Every day you come up with another daft speech about organic prayer books or GM architects or something else you know nothing about.

"Other people might be scared of you, Charles, but not me. I'm going on that march and that's an end to it!"

She spun on her heel and stormed out of the room, slamming the door behind her, a sound that echoed down the corridors of his memory to all those other slammed doors in the past.

Outside in the growing dusk the first leaves of autumn fluttered to the ground, harbingers of the cold winter that was to come...

© Sylvie Krin Airport Romance Series. Enjoy excerpts from her other best-selling titles at www.krintrash.com

TORIES' NEW PLAN

by Our Political Staff **Peter O'Bore**

THE CONSERVATIVE Party has announced a radical new five-point plan to win back the hearts and minds of its disenchanted supporters.

That Plan In Full

1. Introduction of a so-called "Welfare State", guaranteeing state benefits "from the cradle to the grave".
2. A "National Health Service" with healthcare free at the point of delivery – including glasses and false teeth.
3. Nationalisation of key industries, such as the railways, bringing them under state control.
4. Conservative Party to be renamed "Old Labour".
5. Iain Duncan Smith to change name to Iain Nye-Bevan.

Late News

Michael Foot To Join Tories Shock **94**

"I'm ringing about this dishwasher I bought from you yesterday"

MᶜLACHLAN

London Fashion Week

TONY is wearing this autumn's smartest outfit. From the "Man At CIA" range, Tony is sporting waist-hugging "Dubya" chinos with matching no-nonsense "Bible" belt, topped with a stylish "Bushman" jacket and special "Historic Tie". The look that says "Let's Kick Ass". Perfect for town and desert wear.

BOY IS 18 SHOCK

by Our Entire Staff

A YOUNG schoolboy celebrated his 18th birthday yesterday (Reuters).

On Other Pages

● 100s of pictures of 18-year-old boy **2-21**

● What happens when a boy becomes 18 by Dr Thomas Stutterford **22**

● What other famous people looked like when they were 18 **22-38**

● Get yourself a hair-style like the 18-year-old boy **38**

PLUS

What The 18-Year-Old Can Now Do Legally

● **He can drink in a pub surrounded by loads of paparazzi photographers.**

● He can run past hordes of paparazzi photographers to see an 18 film.

● **Move into a new home which is completely ringed by hundreds of paparazzi photographers.**

● Drive very fast through the streets of Paris whilst being chased by hordes of paparazzi... *(Er... that's enough things Harry can legally do. Ed.)*

School news

St Cakes

Obesity Term begins today. There is only room for three boys in the school. J.N. Lard-Bucket (Dumplings) is Senior Fatso. B. Bunter (Porkers) is Scoffer of the Pies. There will be no run this year over Founders Meadow, following medical advice. The new McDonald's Wing for Catering Studies will be opened by the Right Hon. Nicholas Soames (O.C.) on November 3rd. There will be a performance of "Hello, Mr Chips" in the school dining room every day, sponsored by McCain's Oven Ready Fries. The Founder's Day Dinner will be held in the tuck shop on St Cake's Day on 23rd November. Coronaries will be on December 3rd.

THINGS TO DO WITH YOUR KIDS

No. 94

If your kids are bored with school, why not take them out on a day trip to the local magistrates court?

Hours of fun can be had painting colourful placards reading "String 'em up", creating nooses to wave, and banging on the top of vans screaming "Rot in Hell you scum".

Children will love it and it's educational too, introducing them to concepts of justice at an early age (National Curriculum Key Stage 7(b)(iii)).

Check local press for details of upcoming court appearances of accused.

Match the Celebs with their Toothbrush

by Polly Filling

PSYCHIATRISTS have long known that our choice of toothbrush says more about us than we think. The subtle combination of handle and brush, the choice between electric and water-fuelled, between curved and straight – these are seminal indicators of the true person within.

Can you match our chosen celebrities with their toothbrush? Your solution could earn you and your partner a life supply of Harrods Homebrand Toothpaste (as used by Mohamed al Fugger).

Now turn to page 94 for the correct answers.

A. No sweeties, Sweetie, or your teeth won't look ABSOLUTELY FABULOUS!

B. This celebrity's toothbrush isn't as POSH as his wife's!

C. Does my gum look big in this, ANDREW?!

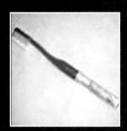

D. STEVE gave this famous toothbrusher the BRUSH OFF!

E. AHEM, this has more bristles than its owner's head!

F. AND FINALLY... whose toothbrush is this?!